Not On My Watch

The 21st Century Combat Medic

By

Joshua M. Peters and
Josh R. Fansler

Foreword by
Congressman Mike Pence

authorHOUSE™

1663 LIBERTY DRIVE, SUITE 200
BLOOMINGTON, INDIANA 47403
(800) 839-8640
WWW.AUTHORHOUSE.COM

First published by AuthorHouse 12/14/04

ISBN: 1-4208-1145-2 (sc)
ISBN: 1-4208-1146-0 (dj)

Library of Congress Control Number: 2004099208

Printed in the United States of America
Bloomington, Indiana

This book is printed on acid-free paper.

July 2019

Table of Contents

Dedication

I was a youngster near ten years of age when one day I noticed a sign hanging in the gym during one of my gymnastic meets. The sign read, "It is never too late to welcome home a Vietnam Vet." Although only ten, I did know a little about the Vietnam War. I could tell you where Vietnam was on a map. I also knew that my parents had friends and business colleagues who fought in that terrifying war. I new of key places such as Saigon, Hanoi, and the Ho Chi Minh Trail, but what I didn't understand in 1990, a good number of years after that war had ended, was why would a Vietnam veteran still need welcomed home? I asked my mother about the sign on our way out the door after the meet. She said to me, "When the troops came home from Vietnam in the 60's and 70's they were booed and shouted at by Americans protesting the war. Occasionally they were spit on and had things thrown at them. It was terrible that citizens of this country turned their backs on the Soldiers. That is why it is never too late to welcome home a Vietnam Vet."

Now, fourteen years later, I still believe strongly in the message my mother conveyed to me that day and to the image of that old white sign written in bright red ink hanging from the rafters of the gym. I have also realized that it is never too late to welcome home and to thank any veteran. I love my freedom - and I will never forget those who served before me and with me. It is those Soldiers who preserved my freedom and the freedom of our great nation.

To the families who have sacrificed so much by saying goodbye to sons and daughters, husbands and wives, and brothers and sisters.

To every man and woman who has answered the call to duty.

To the Soldiers, Sailors, Airmen, and Marines who stand guard day and night to protect our great nation.

And to the Medics and Medical Service Officers who creed, *"Not on my watch."*

God Bless You and God Bless America.

Foreword

When Specialist Joshua Peters and Specialist Josh Fansler approached me about the possibility of writing the forward to the book you now hold in your hands, I was deeply humbled. These men represent the finest tradition of American military service and I was honored to have the opportunity to endorse your consideration of this work. As you read through the following pages I think you will understand why I was humbled by the request, and why I gladly agreed to do it.

The Bible reads that if you owe debts, pay debts; if honor, then honor; if respect, then respect. And so it is with grateful heart that I am pleased to recognize the authentic contribution of the authors and to honor the men and women of Operation Iraqi Freedom and Operation Enduring Freedom.

As a Member of Congress, I traveled to Operation Iraqi Freedom on two separate occasions. While my visits included meetings with top military leaders and the leaders of the new Interim Iraqi Government, it was my time spent with ordinary Soldiers on the ground that made me realize the nature of the sacrifice which so many American families have made on behalf of the freedom of the Iraqi people and the worthiness of our mission in the global war on terror.

Like the authors of this book, these are men and women committed to the defense of the freedoms and ideals we as Americans rightly hold so dear, and they prove that commitment by placing their lives on the line every day for these ideals. Theirs is a noble work, and they go about it with pride and skill.

And this book is the story of those who serve those who serve. The story of the modern Army Medic is a timely tale and will help students of warfare and the citizens of our nation better understand the challenges our military will face in the difficult days ahead and the valor of those who render the medical assistance which that service too often demands.

The authors of this book are men who have proved their worth. The courage of the men of this book has saved lives. I think you will agree with me that this book is compelling, informative and timely. As we go forward in confronting our global enemy in the war on terror, I am glad we have such men to look after our brave service men and women who find themselves in harm's way on our behalf.

Rep. Mike Pence
Member of Congress
June 18, 2004

Our Words

What if your entire view of the world was controlled by what someone else showed you? What if your day to day life was limited to only what someone else observed as interesting? What if any blemish of your actions was exposed through a microscope so strong that the entire world would instantly be alerted? What if you were expected to conduct combat operations for twelve months straight under these conditions and still perform to a standard so strict, while an entire nation and region of the globe depended on you and your comrades' ability to cope? We were on the other side of the world view, our lives were viewed only after convoy ambushes and hotel bombings, and our blemishes, although very few and far between, were exposed as national headlines.

A thought-provoking question worthy of debate has been asked of us repeatedly: If the media had had the involvement in World War II as they do in modern warfare, would the Allies have won? The basis of this question stems from the fact that not only Americans, but indeed, the world population are imbedded in the jacket pocket of every military leader up the chain to the President of the United States. Critics stand at every foothold in progress and blast policy and productivity. Hindsight is made into public hearings. Would an up-to-the-second informed public have accepted the great loss of life? Would the American public have been understanding in the dark days, months, yes, even years of the early 1940's?

Afghanistan and Iraq are now more familiar to people than the current events in hometowns all across the country. Yet, the familiarity is from the edited views of a newsroom in New York City or Washington, DC. The good rarely outweighs the bad when the news anchor now comes through the television not only at just the 6 o'clock hour, but continually on 24-hour headline news channels, giving an exacerbated effect to every incident. National opinion sparks firestorms in debate circles and the American Soldier, Sailor, Airman, and Marine overseas bear the harshest burden. This is 21st Century combat.

Along a desolate, desert highway, somewhere between Baghdad and the Kuwaiti border, we decided we must write this book. This was our last convoy after our year-long deployment. On this deserted Iraqi road we had plenty of time for reflection over the past year of combat. We were disturbed by stories our families had told us of the information they'd received back home about the war; most of it entirely inaccurate. We decided we owed it to you, the reader, to tell our story the way it happened.

This book will give you a glimpse into our reasons for joining the Army during wartime. Our story takes you on a journey from our lives before the war to the mountainous terrains of Afghanistan and the barren deserts of Iraq. It is our desire to bring to life what it is like for the American Soldier fighting in the war on terror overseas. Not just from a Soldier's perspective, but from the Combat Medic's perspective. We want you to learn about the heartaches, the fear, the excitement and the terror of combat today. These stories are not intended to bring glory upon ourselves. They are written to show the courage and bravery of every American Soldier with whom we served. While this book is written from our first person view, the "I" and "we" are inclusive of all the Medics that have served Operation Enduring Freedom and Operation Iraqi Freedom. Every medic deployed in support of these operations have similar stories to tell.

The title, "Not On My Watch, The 21st Century Combat Medic" expresses the fervor with which we serve. First, our motto: Not On My Watch. This speaks not only of the personal pride and sacrifice that we, as Combat Medics have in our assignment, but also of our willingness to sacrifice in order to save a fellow Soldier's life. We are saying, "As long as I am there, I am going to sacrifice everything I have to give the wounded Soldier a second chance at life". The latter part of the title stresses how combat and combat medicine has evolved to our generation from the generation of the heroes who served from the very first shot of the Revolutionary War until now.

We have met the men and women of past wars at welcome home ceremonies, the local VFW's, and through everyday interactions. Every story is different, yet every story is exactly the same: The same courage, bravery, honor, and dedication to fellow Soldiers on the battlefield. We remember the look of pride in the eyes of every Vietnam, Korean, and WWII veteran as they shook our hands at the airport upon our arrival back to the United States. It is that look that lets us know that although we never stormed a beach on that Day in June of 1944, or never took that hill in the jungle with certain death on the ascent to the top, we did serve a cause that blankets our great country with Freedom. We are Americans fighting and defending the rights of every American. We are Americans dedicated to bringing peace and democracy to every citizen of the globe. Our cause is just and this is our story.

Combat Medic Prayer

Oh, Lord I ask for your divine strength to meet the demands of my profession. Help me to be the finest medic, both technically and tactically. If I am called to the battlefield, give me the courage to conserve our fighting forces by providing medical care to all who are in need. If I am called to a mission of peace, give me the strength to lead by caring for those who need my assistance. Finally, Lord, help me take care of my own spiritual, physical, and emotional needs. Teach me to trust in your presence and never-failing love. AMEN.

Soldier's Creed

I am an American Soldier.

I am a warrior and member of a team. I serve the people of the United States and live the Army values.

I will always place the mission first.

I will never accept defeat.

I will never quit.

I will never leave a fallen comrade.

I am disciplined, physically and mentally tough, trained and proficient in my warrior tasks and drills. I always maintain my arms, my equipment and myself.

I am an expert and a professional.

I stand ready to deploy, engage and destroy the enemies of the United States of America in close combat.

I am a guardian of freedom and the American way of life.

I am an American Soldier.

The Combat Medic: A History Of Honor

The history of the Combat Medic is rich in pride and tradition. Always prepared to answer the call of a wounded Soldier, the Medic has sworn to conserve the fighting strength. Combat medicine has been readily available to every fighting American since the Revolutionary War. It is most often the Combat Medic that provides the first critical care necessary to save a Soldier's life. It is most often the Combat Medic that provides comfort to the wounded. It is all too often that the Combat Medic hears the last words and wishes of a dying hero.

As man has developed more efficient ways to destroy his enemy, the Combat Medic has risen to the challenge of adapting to these ways and overcoming them when possible. Long gone are the days of blood-soaked tents which provided immediate field amputations. The Civil War left over 50,000 of its veterans with amputations. Their knowledge of diseases and sterility was primitive at best. Countless men died during that war due to sickness and disease. Medical personnel were available to the Soldier, yet the wounded had to wait until he was evacuated to a medic or doctor. At that time, medical personnel did not march side by side with the warriors.

It wasn't until Word War I that the military medic fought right alongside the infantry and other war-fighting units. Due to the large number of casualties, the importance of the medic on the line was becoming quite apparent. After WWI, medics began to receive advanced training not only in combat medicine, but also in soldiering skills. The true grit of the Combat Medic was soon to be tested.

Soldiers wounded in World War II had a survival rate over three times that of Soldiers wounded in the previous war due to this extensive training. While the importance of the highly trained medic on the battlefield grew, so did his value as a target to the enemy. The balance between being a Soldier and being a medic was one that had to be kept at even keel.

The Korean Conflict saw the concept of mobile surgical hospitals and advanced evacuation capabilities such as the helicopter. The time saved transporting patients by air increased the wounded man's chance of survival once again.

The Vietnam War was the first time that medics were able to ride alongside of their patients and provide continuing care while en route to the nearest hospital. It was this conflict that gave birth to the flight medic.

Today, through building on all of the ideas and trials of the previous conflicts, the 21st Century Combat Medic is better prepared and better trained than any medic that had come before him. We are now equipped with advanced airway interventions. We are now trained on bandages, dressings and coagulants that slow down or completely stop severe bleeding within seconds. Our knowledge of intravenous fluids and medication on the battlefield is unparalleled.

Our evacuation of the wounded may be performed through HMMWV ambulances, armored tracked ambulances, and Blackhawk helicopters. We are also trained on how to convert various other vehicles into non-standard medical evacuation vehicles.

Forward Surgical Teams and Combat Support Hospitals now provide fighting Americans with nearly unlimited surgical possibilities within minutes of the injury. This option would not have been afforded to Soldiers as it is now just a decade ago without the foundation built on past experience.

The life-saving capabilities we now have on the battlefield give every United States service member the best second chance at life they have ever had in combat. The 21st Century Combat Medic owes everything to what his fathers learned in the trenches of Europe, the hills of Korea and the jungles of Vietnam.

---SECTION ONE---
By: Josh R. Fansler

INTRODUCTION

Where I Was

Footsteps boomed down the hallway that had lay quiet just moments before. Voices then followed the echo of footsteps as the hallway became louder and louder. The 82nd Airborne Division headquarters was now alive with commotion. The door to the Commanding General's briefing room stood open and through it came the Division's Command Sergeant Major. "Everybody out! The U.S. is under attack! Report back to your units!"

***

One month earlier I had won the 504th Parachute Infantry Regiment Driver of the Year competition; a showcase of military vehicle knowledge and driving skills coupled with a written test and, of course, an in-ranks inspection. It was not a major event; there was no ceremony for winning and no spectators looking on, it was simply a competition between the three battalions of the 504th. It was something a First Sergeant could use to hold over the head of other First Sergeants to display the quality of his Soldiers.

I walked away as the "Brigade Driver of the Year" with a coin and a handshake. Winning also ensured my spot in the Division Driver of the Quarter competition to be held at Division Headquarters on September 11th, 2001.

I reported to Division Headquarters at 0730 to start the competition. My pressed BDUs and highly polished Corcoran Jump Boots stood to be inspected as the first part of the grading process. Unbeknownst to all present, in less than ninety minutes the course of America and the resolve of the American people would be changed forever.

After the in-ranks inspection, we were directed to move into the N+2 room, the Commander's briefing room for every mission the 82nd executed. The room was furnished with giant wooden tables surrounded by leather high back chairs. We all found our seats in the briefing room at around 0830 and began the hundred-question written test. We were given one hour to complete the test. Thirty minutes was all the time we were going to have.

I sat with pencil in hand at 0905 when the silence of the testing room was broken by the Sergeant First Class in charge of the competition. "I don't want to alarm you guys," he said with a noticeable concern in his voice, "but a plane just hit one of the World Trade Center buildings."

My first thought was *how could anyone be so careless as to hit one of the tallest buildings in the world?* I was sure it couldn't have been a commercial airline and that it was probably a single engine private plane that had lost control and crashed into the skyscraper. I told myself that there was nothing to worry about. I put my eyes back on my test and continued scribbling answers.

Moments later, the same Sergeant came running back into the room. "A second plane just hit the other tower! We are under attack!"

Footsteps boomed down the hallway that had lay quiet just moments before. Voices then followed the echo of footsteps as the hallway became louder and louder. The 82nd Airborne Division Headquarters was now alive with commotion. The door to the Commanding General's briefing room stood open and through it came the Division's Command Sergeant Major. "Everybody out! The United States is under attack! Report back to your units!"

On my way out of the building to the parking lot I was met by a swarm of military police vehicles positioning to block all of the entrances. I couldn't drive my HMMWV out because of the road blocks, so I decided to walk back to my aid station. There were swarms of people everywhere. I passed by the Ardennes Street shoppette and made my way into the building to see if the TVs inside the food court were showing the footage. The dining area was packed, as everyone had their eyes focused on the tape of one burning tower and another plane hitting the second WTC building. Word of the attack on the Pentagon and the downed plane in the Pennsylvania field also made its way across the news bulletin. America was under attack.

I sprinted back to my aid station to find the rest of my platoon already sitting on their rucksacks and duffle bags. "Fans," instructed my squad leader, "go get your bags."

For a week straight we sat on our fully packed bags waiting for the word to jump in on whoever was responsible for the attacks. This was the kind of thing for which we meticulously trained.

Rumors of our deployment were around every corner. It would be nine months before we got our chance to exact revenge. The important thing, however, was that we were ready to go the day it happened. We were America's Guard of Honor and it was *our watch*.

CHAPTER ONE

Airborne!

Time on target was quickly approaching. It had been about two and a half hours since I could last feel my legs under the pressure of my seventy pound rucksack. Inside the C-17 airplane sat ninety-nine other jumpers just as anxious as I was to return feeling to their seemingly lifeless limbs. This was just one of many training jumps we performed every year. It was our average two o'clock in the morning, 800 feet above ground level, 600 to 900 paratroopers in the air at the same time, combat simulated, hurry-up-and-get-it-over-with-so-we-can-get-on-with-the-mission-jump. Nothing out of the ordinary.

***

I enlisted in the Army a young 18-year-old kid who had never left the east coast, let alone the country. The Army was a mystery to me. I had signed on to be a Medical Specialist thinking that I'd be some guy running around in hospital whites like it said in the brochure. My military experience would include four enlisted years, some college money, and a hospital; no adventure, nothing dangerous - just like I promised my mom.

But this wasn't enough for me. I couldn't let it go. I needed more. I wanted every badge in the Army on my chest. One day in AIT (Advanced Individual Training) down at Fort Sam Houston, San Antonio, Texas, my life would change – 100% for the better. A Staff Sergeant recruiter showed up in his Class A dress uniform wearing a maroon beret with his pants tucked into his highly polished jump boots. Without knowing what this guy did for a living, my interest was immediately perked.

His hour-long presentation of Airborne School to my entire class of 200 plus students ended with only eleven of us sticking around to put our names on the dotted line. *I was going to get to tuck my Class A pants into my jump boots!*

In March of 2000 I reported to Ft Bragg, North Carolina for my duty assignment to 1st Battalion, 504th Parachute Infantry Regiment. Life in the 504th was tough at best. A demanding schedule coupled with high intensity training, created the backbone of the 82nd's slogan; "Giving the enemy every opportunity to die for his country day or night."

Medics in the 82nd had a very challenging role. We marched, we jumped, we fought side by side with the rifleman, and through it all we were expected to maintain the highest standard of medical care. There were times that my rucksack outweighed most infantryman packs by at least thirty to thirty five pounds. I hurt, froze, and sucked it up, but through it all, I became a Combat Medic. It now became so much more than a uniform change; it was a way of life.

The 82nd taught me how to grow. It was the first real chapter of my adult life. I will forever be an 'Airborne Medic.'

CHAPTER TWO

Oops, My Bad!

Nothing clouds the thoughts of a deployed Soldier more than getting the hell home. So naturally, just about every conversation deals with what you're going to do when you get back home, how you miss the fun times of your adolescence, and the estimations of exactly how many beers you will be able to drink before total inebriation sets in. You have these conversations with everybody even if you've never met them before. It helps to pass the time and before you know it you're laughing like old friends. These conversations were especially valuable during the eight hours of guard duty we had to pull every day on the border town of Lwara, Afghanistan in October of 2002. Fittingly, the name of our base was "Fire Base Lwara" and it sat atop a hill surrounded on three sides by mountains and only a stone's throw away from Pakistan to the west. Our base served an important objective because it was on a main weapons smuggling route for the Taliban and Al Qaeda from Pakistan into the heart of Afghanistan. However, our importance couldn't have been judged by mere observance. "Fire Base Lwara" was about the size of two football fields and manned by seventy Army and Army Special Forces personnel at any given time.

The mountains to our east, south, and west towered over us and were prime areas from which the enemy could launch attacks. The only advantage of our position was that each side of our hill was surrounded by razor wire and steeped at about fifty degrees. Being about one hundred meters to the top made any foot attack on us nearly impossible. A buddy of mine and I once concurred that we could most likely suppress an attack of 150 enemy personnel before we would become overwhelmed. On each side of the hill we had a "bunker" position where two personnel would pull guard duty.

The 'bunkers' were only called bunkers because calling them "worthless holes in the ground covered by plywood and a couple of sand bags" didn't give us the same sense of security. It wasn't unusual for one of the bunkers to collapse, leaving the two Soldiers on guard to perform their duty standing outside the crumble of sand that once was their shelter from incoming fire. So it was that in these bunkers we would sit guard for eight hours a day, having our conversations about home and trying not to commit the mortal sin of looking at our watches.

The watch is an adversary unto itself during guard duty; second only to the enemy themselves. Eight hours is a long time to sit and stare at the same mountain and have the same conversation for the fifth time that month, yet while doing that, believing that time must be burning by. In my head at least three hours have gone by, but the moment I look at my watch, I realize that only half that time has really elapsed. Time is a killer.

To the west of our hilltop base was a dry riverbed, also known as a "road" to the people of Lwara and most of Afghanistan. This "road", which ran to Pakistan, was our main focus to catch smugglers. Therefore, we had a traffic control point (TCP) set up right below Bunker One. On duty at our TCP were three members of the Afghan Military Force (AMF), a small band of militia men hired by the US military to provide local security until that Afghan National Army (ANA) could be recruited, trained, and put into action. While the members of the AMF seemed to be a proud bunch and were amiable enough during our interactions, they could be trusted about as far as they could be thrown. Allowing them to control the TCP was mostly a way of keeping an eye on them while also keeping them gainfully employed.

There was a night in October when I found myself on guard in Bunker One directly above the AMF checkpoint. Earlier in the evening we had been advised that the city of Lwara had been placed on curfew, forbidding the townspeople from driving at night. The reason for the curfew was that intelligence had been gathered that led us to believe there was a shipment of weapons crossing the border that night. Therefore, every vehicle was to be considered a target and it was to be stopped and searched or, in the event of noncompliance, to be dealt with accordingly. Our orders on guard were to signal at any sign of movement down the riverbed road so that the quick reaction force (QRF), consisting of two tan HMMWVs, each manned by four Soldiers, could be notified and directed to the suspects.

So, there I sat in my Kevlar body armor holding my M-4 rifle, complete with M-203 grenade launcher attached at the barrel and my night vision goggles around my neck, securely in my bunker, listening to the other Soldier on guard with me tell me how many beers he'll have when he gets back to Ft. Bragg in January, and of course staring at the mountains in Pakistan. I thought to myself that it had to have been at least two hours since we started our guard duty and it was killing me not to take a glance at my watch. All I could think was that it was dark, cold, and boring. Every now and then I would take a look down at the AMF checkpoint and see the three men standing around their burn barrel staying warm and wishing we could start a fire up here to be just as warm. My mind would drift from one event in my life to the next. I would think about the guys who had survived our past wars and how they would look at what I'm doing and tell me that this is not a real war. I would think about how I wanted to see some action just so I could have some stories to tell when I got home. Little did I know that in the coming months and years I would see all that action and wish I hadn't asked for any of it when I was sitting in my bunker bored to death.

But there I sat, my mind still wondering a little further down memory lane, when the sight of three sets of headlights caught my vision.

"Oh, shit," I thought as I scrambled myself upright, *this could be the one.*

"Hey, did you see that?" I asked the other Soldier on guard. He was already looking for the field phone to call the command post.

Without answering me, he handed me the phone and said, "Call it in."

"Fire a flare," was the response I received from the other end of the field phone.

"What did he say?" he asked when I put the black phone back on the receiver.

"Uuhh, he said, 'fire a flare.'...Dude, where the hell is the flare?"

After a few seconds of scrambling around in the dark, he handed me the flare, "Here you go, Doc." The white phosphorous flare was a metal cylinder about the size of a paper towel roll that has a "knurled" hand grip and stuff that goes 'boom' in the middle.

I had never fired a flare before...I had never even held a flare before. Good thing everything that the military produces has instructions printed on it. So there I sat with the flare in my left hand and my blue mini light in my right hand reading the easy-to-follow directions to employ a flare.

Step 1. Remove blasting cap from top of flare. *Okay, easy enough,* I thought to myself.

2. Place blasting cap at the bottom of flare. *Okay, I can do this.*

3. Grip flare by knurled end with right hand.

Okay, what the hell is a knurled end? "Dude, what the hell is a knurled end?" I asked again this time out loud. Damn these easy step by step instructions!

Seconds later, I have my right hand gripping the knurled, textured end of the flare tube.

4. With arm extended, either slam the flare down on a hard surface or strike up on the blasting cap with left hand.

Now, this is where things always go bad for me – they have given me a choice. In my experience with choices I have usually made the wrong one. I choose the line on the left, the line on the right moves faster, I choose the chicken meal on the airplane, and the beef looks better, and so on. So, I quickly do some logical thinking and I decide that if I strike the flare on a hard surface, I will most likely be aiming it at my eye when it goes 'boom'. I have made my decision and I will be striking it with my left hand – that shouldn't be so bad right?

'BOOM' keeps going through my mind. I am now standing outside the bunker, right leg in front of my left, right arm extended holding the flare, ballistic helmet on with my NVGs attached to the top, and my left arm taking warm-up swings at the blasting cap.

"Hit it, Doc," I hear from the bunker.

Hindsight is a wonderful thing. It is the "shoulda, woulda, coulda" of what may have transpired had I done something differently. Hindsight in this case would have me hit the flare on a hard surface rather than my hand. Hindsight in this case could have prevented the tremendous pain in my left hand from the force of the blast that I was unprepared for. Hindsight in this case should have fired the flare into the air where it is intended to be fired to serve its purpose, rather than directly at the AMF checkpoint down the hill from where I was standing. Hindsight would have kept the white phosphorous from burning down the tent that the AMF soldiers were so comfortably standing in just seconds before.

"Doc," one of the guys says to me the next day, "what kind of weapon do you carry?"

"An M-4 with an M-203 grenade launcher," I responded realizing exactly where this conversation was going as I nursed my still aching hand.

"Doc, why didn't you fire a flare from your 203?" he said with a smirk on his face.

Hindsight!!

CHAPTER THREE

The Business End of the Gun

The Chinese-made 107mm Rocket created quite a stir at Lwara Fire Base. So did the A-10 warthogs and AC-130 gunship that we called in to destroy them the night Taliban insurgents decided to fire them at us from a mountainside west of our bases' hilltop position.

October 14th, 2002 found me sitting in another dirt bunker facing west into Pakistan. The four-hour guard shift was dragging by with the same conversations of home and future plans. There was little moonlight as the vast darkness covered the valley and mountains. Every couple of nights our mortar team would fire illumination rounds to break the pitch black to serve the purpose of telling the enemy, "Hey we're here and we're always awake, don't try anything stupid."

Two hours into my stay at the bunker retreat, there was a huge explosion to our rear. I spun around thinking that one of the mortar tubes had exploded, but there was no activity behind us.

What the hell was that? I thought before asking the same question out loud.

"Did you see anything?" I asked the infantryman on duty with me.

He shrugged his shoulders and picked up the thermal imaging device to scan our perimeter.

The Staff Sergeant assigned as Sergeant of the Guard (SOG) came sprinting to our position not one minute after the explosion. "Where did that rocket come from?"

Rocket? "I...I don't know." I told him honestly as I finally realized that we were under attack. The three of us began to scan the mountainsides for any sign of the rocket launch site. A few moments later, a brilliant flash came from the mountain we had taken to calling 'crooked tree' because of the lone tree that perched at the top at a 45-degree angle.

"Incoming!" The three of us shouted in unison as another rocket propelled at our base. The sound of the explosive heading at us was unmistakable: The screaming, "Fssstwaaaack – BOOM."

"Doc," screamed the SOG, "shoot an azimuth to that position and call it in to the command post."

I already had my compass in hand along with the range card for our bunker when he gave me the instruction. "I'm on it."

I ducked low against the dirt and sandbag front wall of the bunker as I shot my azimuth toward where the rockets were being launched, knowing that the 'bunker' would do very little to protect us if one of the 107s decided to pay us a visit. "88 degrees," I shouted as another rocket slammed into the side of our hill kicking up a cloud of dust and stones.

"Call it in to the CP (command post/command point)!" rang out his next instructions.

Another rocket came screaming at us, this time louder than the three previous. "Incoming!" The sound traveled right over our heads and exploded in the valley behind our hill.

"CP this is Bunker Three" I spoke into the TA-312 field telephone after the guard in the CP had answered. "I've got an azimuth and distance on the launch site."

"Send it," came the frantic response.

"88 degrees at about twenty to twenty-five-hundred meters from my position."

"Roger, good copy," he said then hung up.

More rockets came slamming into our hill, each with the distinctive scream and earth-shaking explosion. I could hear the mortars readying to fire a few meters behind me. My heart was pounding through my chest.

The mortars finally opened up on the assault. I concentrated on the mountainside to visualize hits on target. But the mortars never hit the intended 88 degrees at 2500 meters. Instead, they were fired northwest into a farmer's field. *What the hell are they firing at?* I thought before shouting it out loud over the booms.

"CP this is Bunker Three!" I shouted into the field phone. "Cease fire, cease fire, you are way off the mark! 88 degrees, I say again, 88 degrees at 2500 meters!"

After dropping seven or eight errant rounds way off the mark, the mortar tubes ceased firing. Everyone else in the base was against the perimeter sandbags with rifles fixed on the launch site. Radio reports indicated zero injuries - only a few close calls. The best news: " An AC-130 gunship and A-10s are en route on the position."

We braced for more impacts as we kept a close eye on the mountainside. No one blinked for fear of missing another attempted attack. The gunship and A-10s were audible in the distance behind us to the southeast. I flipped down my NVGs (Night Vision Goggles) to witness the spectacle through the green tint of night vision. *Those poor bastards have no idea what they're in for if they were dumb enough to stick around,* I thought as the A-10s moved within range.

The A-10's piercing sound of rounds spitting from the mouth of the flying beast, sent a spine-tingling surge down the necks of everyone watching from our hilltop position. The AC-130 then joined in with precision blasts from his mounted cannon, spraying the target with deadly accuracy. The runs continued for the better half of one hour before heading home with our debt of gratitude in tow.

As soon as the planes finished their bombardment of the mountainside, we launched our QRF (Quick Reaction Force) to a home perceived to be the get-away point for the insurgents. Forty-five minutes later, they returned with two men in custody. The duo was covered in rocket grease with traces of propellant. They also had fuses in their possession. They pleaded their innocence but, upon realizing we had all the evidence, conceded their guilt.

The enemy had attacked on my watch, but they could not escape the watch of the United States military.

CHAPTER FOUR

The Americans Brought the Doctors, We Brought the Countryside

Throughout the many operations, in the history of the United States military, both war and peacekeeping, winning the hearts and minds of the local population has served as a fantastic source of information. We provide a service for the people, and then they do something for us. Sincerity on our part is the key to earning the trust and confidence we need from the community.

Before each major movement or operation in Afghanistan, psychological operations, or Psy-Ops for short, would print flyers stating the goals of our mission in that particular village. It would lay out our prospects of finding members of Al-Qaeda or the ousted Taliban regime, stating that any and all help from the villagers in apprehending these individuals would move the village one step closer to freedom and prosperity. One of the major incentives for help from the local people during our missions was called MEDCAPing. It was promised to the villagers that with their complete cooperation during an operation, that afterwards, medics and doctors would tend to the sick members of the community.

Each operation found us screening and treating villagers from minor headaches and pains to complaints of sand flea leishmaniasis. We gave the children multi-vitamin pills and well-child exams, adults were provided with antibiotics and analgesics, and all members of the village were given brochures written in Arabic on proper medical practices to remain healthy.

The town of Organ-E, just northwest of Kandahar, proved to be a much more trying MEDCAP than we had thought. We had occupied a forward operating base on the west side of the town since the beginning of our tour in Afghanistan. The base was a refuel point for all helicopter travels north of Kandahar and storage cache for numerous rockets and mortar fired explosives that we had confiscated. I called a cot in a cold tent at Organ-E home from mid-November 2002 to January 2003. The villagers had cooperated with all of our missions in the town and we even employed members of the town on our base, so we decided that we would offer our medical services to every citizen of the town as a display of our gratitude.

The day before our humanitarian medical screening was scheduled, we posted a letter to notify the locals. It encouraged the townspeople to come to our front gates at 0700 local time where they would be screened and treated by Army doctors, PAs, and Medics.

Shortly after breakfast on the morning of the MEDCAP, I walked down to the front gates with Staff Sergeant Bereiter to help with the process. We were unprepared for the vast amount of people forming the line waiting for the chance to see an American doctor. The line stretched for approximately a mile with more locals joining in every minute. We were expecting only about six-hundred. It was going to be a long day.

Promptly at seven the gates opened and our patients started pouring in. We had three treatment tents set up; two for males and children and one for females. We saw everything from broken bones that were days and weeks old to chronic aches and pains. We were certain that a lot of people just saw a line and stood in it not knowing what it was for because many of the people we saw were completely healthy. Old men with two wooden legs because of wounds suffered during the war with Russia, came in seeking new prosthetics. We did the best we could for as many of the people as we could. We had succeeded in winning their hearts and minds. The day was long and it expanded into the night. We saw every local national that came to our gates that day. We gave everyone a new hope. It was *our watch*.

CHAPTER FIVE

Out of the Frying Pan, Into the Fire

Afghanistan was the awakening of a lifetime. It was my introduction to a culture that I had only read about. I also learned more about myself than I ever thought possible. An ancient Chinese philosopher once said, "You can know a man for thirty years, spending every day with him. But hold that man to the edge of a volcano, and for the first time you will really meet him." This Afghanistan deployment seemed to be of this volcanic experience, however, I was soon to find that my future deployment to Iraq would be yet the very edge of the burning pit of lava. I would finally meet the real me. I would be tested even more in the year to come. I swore that no matter what, it would always be my watch.

I left the 82nd Airborne Division in March of 2003 and was en route to Fort Carson, Colorado after my six months in the deserts and mountains of Afghanistan. My choice to re-enlist came with the knowledge of a huge movement of troops into Iraq, of which I was more than certain I would be a part. I knew little of the units that called Ft. Carson home, but trusted that I would be able to

adapt to any mission they were called on to accomplish. My orders:
The Third Armored Cavalry Regiment.

I arrived at my unit a light infantry Soldier, accustomed to survival from the supplies I carried on my back, thrown into a whole new game of heavy track vehicles and trucks. I was told that I had one week to get acclimated before deploying with the main body on April 9th, three days after my one year wedding anniversary. It was a week full of stress and tears, but I had the assurance from my beautiful wife, Katie, that she would be able to cope. Her strength was my strength as I kissed her goodbye for the second time in less than eight months. Her only fear was the lack of bonds I had with the troopers of my new unit. When I left for Afghanistan, I was with good friends. They would, with no questions asked, risk their lives for me as I would have done the same for them. Her comfort level this time was nowhere near as great. I assured her that I would have those same bonds here in no time. I made true on my promise.

SPC Josh Fansler is reunited with his wife Katie after returning to the United States from Afghanistan.

CHAPTER SIX

Wrong Way Down A One Way Street

"Doc, hey doc," the voice called through the darkness and chill of late spring.

I tried to sleep through it, imagining it was only voices in my dream and not me actually being awakened in the middle of the night. Although it was only a couple of days short of May, sleeping outside still required our medium weight sleeping bag to keep warm until the sun burned through in the hot Iraq morning. I did not want to leave the comfort of my bag this night.

"Doc, doc, there was an accident, wake up."

"Fans, you up?" asked the doctor, Major Greg Leigh, who had also been awakened by the voices.

"Yeah, sir, I'm awake. What's going on?"

We were informed that there had been a head-on collision between two Iraqi civilian cars about two miles down the highway from our side-of-the-road base cluster on Highway 8. "We have three dead and three others pretty jacked up," informed the voice again.

The other medic with me, Sergeant Ned Walters, and the doctor, MAJ Leigh, both hopped in the four litter ambulance HMMWV as I fired it up while still trying to tie my boots and fasten my body armor vest. This was going to be our first taste of action since crossing into Iraq from Kuwait just a week earlier. For that entire week we had been sitting at a rest stop on the side of Highway 8 about 40 miles south of Baghdad with no perimeter, no observation posts, and no communication with any of our other cavalry elements. The responsibility of the roughly 30 personnel at this location was to provide logistical support for our units moving north as they passed through our checkpoint. It was also our responsibility to provide medical support for the checkpoint and any other call that came across our radios. There had been no need for us up until this point. It was 'Go time' and we were ready.

Speeding against the oncoming traffic lane of Highway 8 while trying to keep the lead HMMWV in sight, my mind began to evoke my training; airway, breathing, circulation. Airway, breathing, circulation: The three most important pieces of saving or maintaining a person's life. I started to visualize the accident scene and going over the types of injuries to be expected.

Two miles down the road, we met a yellow Chevy four-door and we screeched to a halt. The three of us jumped onto the pavement and spread out to three of the doors. The stench of blood and alcohol was putrid as the stagnant air from inside of the mangled car mixed with the night air. 'Jacked up' was the correct observation from the Soldier that had informed us of the accident. Two of the Iraqis were unconscious with varying degrees of other injuries, and the third was bleeding severely from the head and his left leg was dislocated at the hip and knee. The latter was doing enough screaming for the three of them. *At least he had an airway.*

SGT Walters and MAJ Leigh went to work on the two unconscious patients as I tried to move my way into the vehicle over the blood-soaked rear seat. "Doctor, doctor, help me," and "Doctor, doctor, water," was all my patient could say in his broken English over alcohol-laden breath.

I maneuvered over to fit a C-collar around his neck and his breath caught me through one of his many coughing fits. *Great, tuberculosis - just what I need.* His screaming persisted as I bandaged his forehead, "Doctor, doctor my leg." *What a mess.*

By this time a few townspeople had made their way over to witness the events unfolding in their backyards. I grabbed one of the locals and told him to keep talking to my patient. He shrugged an 'I don't understand you' type shrug at my instructions but had a look of 'I want to help' on his face. So like most people do to break a language barrier, I shouted my instructions again. Yeah, screaming doesn't make people understand! So next I tried hand gestures. "You," I pointed at him, "keep him talking," I started a mouth moving motion with my fingers and thumbs on both hands. He nodded his head very understandingly this time, but just as I gained confidence in my international sign-language skills he reached for a water bottle and offered it to my patient. "No," I shouted, "no, no, no... you know what, just forget it." My frustration returned ten-fold.

On the other side of the car, MAJ Leigh and SGT Walters were having an easier time with their non-responsive patients. The "fat man" as we took to calling him in our identification of the three patients was out-cold, asleep with a fractured upper left arm and a protruding abdomen. Not to mention he probably tipped the scales at three-hundred plus pounds. The other unconscious patient was in much worse shape. His head had impacted the windshield of the car and the force of the blow left his skull feeling like a wet sponge. He was still breathing, but it was his brain's last ditch effort at life. As long as he was alive, he would still be treated as such.

"Hey Sir, I need some help getting our English speaker out of the back of the car."

The two of us worked his skinny body onto a backboard through more cries of pain. His breath continued to reek of inebriation and the coughing continued. His right leg looked completely helpless as it lay turned 90 degrees out of normal position. When we finally got him clear of the car and onto the awaiting litter, we did our best to support the painful lower extremity with splints and blankets. Pulses could be felt distally on all limbs so we loaded him up in the back of the ambulance.

We then turned our attention to the fat man who lay snoring on the ground. Ned had been able to splint and sling the deformed arm which left us only with the obstacle of getting his 300-pound frame onto a litter. Enlisting the help of local bystanders, while making completely sure they understood our instructions, we managed to lift our patient onto a litter. The next challenge that arose was getting him into the back of the ambulance. After finally managing to secure him inside, exhaustion started creeping in on my already tired body.

Our last patient, the Iraqi with the massive skull injury, was a much easier loading task. My only fear was that he would not make the trip to the field hospital. We had kept him alive this long; he was not going to die on us now.

Once all three were loaded, we took off en route to the 21st CSH (Combat Support Hospital). I drove once again with SGT Walters in the passenger seat and MAJ Leigh in the back with our three patients. The trip was long and bumpy over dark highway and rural streets. The aspect of the drive that really scared me was that none of us really had any idea where the 21st CSH was. We had a general idea of the location and a strip map, but finding it was going to be a shot in the dark. *Literally.*

Every bump in the road elicited a moan from our patient with the skull fracture. Every mile or two, the English speaker cried out for water. All the while, the fat man slept in his alcohol-induced slumber. These were our DUI poster boys.

I continued to speed down the pitch black road counting perpendicular streets and landmarks for direction on when and where to turn. Our radio still had no luck reaching anyone that could offer help in finding the CSH. Just over an hour had passed when a sign in the middle of the sand pointed us to LSA Dogwood, the location of the 21st.

"Five minutes, Sir," I called back to MAJ Leigh. "Is our head injury still hanging on?"

"He's still moaning after each bump," he quipped back, insisting that my driving skills left something to be desired.

We finally reached the CSH after passing through two security checkpoints and about ten speed bumps inside the compound. The barbed wire perimeter of the hospital was guarded so once again we needed to pass through a checkpoint. The logistics of this particular checkpoint vexed me because had anyone made it through the first two, the whole base would have been compromised anyway. The guards on duty seemed to realize this fact too, because when we pulled up to the wire, they were both asleep. I sounded my horn to rouse their attention and to make them keenly aware that there was a guy about to die in the back of my ambulance.

After a moment of waiting for the guards to allow me to pass through the gate, I grew annoyed and shouted, "Hey, I've got a guy about to die on me. I'm going through to the ER." The guards' response was his index finger in the air indicating that I should wait a moment. I didn't have any more moments to wait so I responded with a finger of my own and said, "You want me to stop, you'll have to shoot, because I'm going through." And with that, I hit the gas and didn't stop until I reached the tent that read 'ER'.

An hour after we started the drive we had finally reached our destination with all three patients still alive and a pissed-off guard on duty at the gate. We were greeted at the entrance to the ER by a Second Lieutenant that immediately started chewing me out for my actions at the gate.

"You know that my guards could have opened fire on you."

"Yeah, if they had been awake," I shot back. "Are you going to take my patients or what?"

He seemed completely disinterested with the fact we had three people in critical condition in the back of the FLA. His badgering continued until he was joined by a Major who, upon seeing MAJ Leigh and realizing they went to medical school together, stopped the fussing and agreed to take our patients.

The Iraqi with the massive head injury died shortly after reaching the hospital. His brain function was reduced to breathing in and breathing out; the decision was made to take him off life support. The fat man had a ruptured spleen and a fracture to the top of the long bone in the arm where it meets the shoulder. Surgery saved his life. The English speaker was treated for his fractured arm, head injury, and dislocated knee and hip. They were very lucky that all three of them didn't end up in the morgue.

***

It turned out that the three locals involved in the crash were members of the family whose land our rest stop position was located on. The next day the elder of the family came to thank us for our help in the matter and offered us an invitation into his home. Not wanting to appear rude, MAJ Leigh accepted the offer and told the gentleman that we'd be over the next morning before we left to move north. The Iraqi, whose name, quite familiarly, was Ali Muhammad, was extremely happy we agreed to the invitation.

The next morning MAJ Leigh and I made the walk to Ali's house where we were welcomed and treated like dignitaries. They served us a breakfast of eggs, flat bread, potatoes, salted cucumbers, and chi tea. Conversations on everything from politics to music roared throughout the large entertaining area. They spoke to us of a new hope for Iraq and the Middle East.

Ali told us, "Islam is peace. Christianity is peace. And together there will be peace."

We all agreed in the hope that peace would soon comfort the people of Iraq.

Before we left, we were again thanked for our service in helping the three men injured in the accident. They held no ill will about the fact that one of their family members had died. They were just happy to see that our care extended beyond treating our own people. We assured them that it was our job and we would care for and treat all those who needed it. After all, it was *our watch*.

CHAPTER SEVEN

Not On Our Watch

We were ready for three American Soldiers, all KIA (Killed in Action). The radio transmission had been very clear. We were going to meet at the front gate, receive the bodies, ID the bodies, wrap them up and send them off on the incoming helicopters. The M113 track vehicle whipped through the crowd of Soldiers gathered at the gate and around the front gate guard, leaving black skid marks as the rear of the 11 ton vehicle slid into place right in front of us. There was a trail of engine coolant and other fluids gushing from the engine compartment onto the hot August pavement. The heavy armored ramp dropped down with a thunderclap at our feet. KIAs don't scream. Inside the armored beast lay three American Soldiers screaming in a river of crimson; suddenly we were in business and the game clock was running down.

***

"Damn it," I thought out loud to PFC Ricky Becktel, "How many more guys do we have to lose?" I asked rhetorically after we were told about the three Soldiers killed just outside of our base in Al Habbaniyah, Iraq. We were dispatched to the front gate to pick up the three bodies of Soldiers who had just been engaged by insurgents with rocket propelled grenades and AK-47s. The radio was buzzing with traffic about the engagement as everyone involved relayed information and coordinates. Our M1 Abrams tanks and M113-A3 armored personnel carriers raced past us towards the front gate to ensure no other attacks were carried out on the element that was bringing the bodies back to our base.

The buzz over the radio intensified when a voice added new information to the transmissions, "...I say again, we have three wounded en route to the front gate." No sooner had the words broken through the speaker box, than we were joined at the front gate by the rest of the medics working in the aid station; twelve of us in all, plus the Physician's Assistant (PA).

Ordinarily, such a large number of medics working on three patients would have created a chaotic scene. The twelve of us, however, worked like a well-oiled machine when the ramp hit the ground.

The last call we received told us the three casualties were about two minutes away. We had already prepped by laying out all the medical supplies; litters, oxygen, and anything else we would need for the patients when they arrived. We still had in our heads that the KIAs would be coming in first, followed by the three wounded. That idea was quickly put to rest when we saw three Soldiers, all alive, all covered in blood and sweat, and all three with an amputated or partially-amputated leg.

The M113-A3 armored personnel carrier had been on a routine patrol with elements of the 43rd Engineer Battalion through a village near Al Habbaniyah, north of Al Fallujah. Later details told of an ambush on the patrol by insurgents with various small arms weapons and RPG's. In the firefight that ensued, one of the insurgents launched a grenade from the shoulder-fired weapon, piercing the armor and traveling through the inside of the track, injuring the three Soldiers inside. The vehicle, while heavily damaged, continued to run despite the blast to the engine. The medic on scene at the ambush immediately put himself in harm's way, leaving his vehicle to run to the aid of the three injured Soldiers. He was engaged by AK-47 fire from a hilltop forcing him to drop his aid bag and return fire. Once he completed firing, he pulled himself into the track and administered aid to the three Soldiers, starting tourniquets on all three of their badly injured legs. If not for the quick reactions and personal courage of the medic on patrol with the group, the KIA message would have been correct.

The first Soldier we pulled from the track was missing his right leg from the knee level. SGT Hanson and I lifted his body onto a litter and carried him the fifteen feet back to where our medical supplies were laid out. Since there were two of us, and plenty of medics to see to the other causalities, we immediately began our work to keep our Soldier alive. SGT Hanson positioned himself on the right of the patient and immediately applied a second tourniquet to the still bleeding lower limb. I grabbed my trauma shears and began to expose the left side of the Soldiers' body, searching for a vein to establish an intravenous infusion.

Our wounded Soldier was no longer screaming and began to lose color in his face and hands. *Shock.* The A-B-C's of medicine state:

A-airway, B-breathing, C-circulation, and treat for shock. Shock is a medic's biggest enemy - Shock kills. The signs and symptoms of shock must be recognized quickly and treated even faster if a patient is to survive. Our man had an airway, was breathing, and his heart was pumping, but if an IV could not be established within the next precious seconds to counteract the blood lost from his wounds, he would enter a state of irreversible shock and ultimately die.

As his state of shock increased, the veins in his arms began to lose blood-flow, causing collapse. One shot was all I was going to have to get the 14-gauge catheter into his depleting blood stream to combat the onset of further shock. Seconds later, the 1000 milliliter IV bag was flowing fluid into his system. About three minutes later, as the bag emptied its contents into his circulatory system, color returned to his ghostly face and he began to scream. We were not going to lose this patient.

We were then joined by another medic who quickly began to take pulse, blood pressure, and other vital signs. SGT Hanson continued to treat the wounded limb, ensuring that there would be no further blood loss. I exposed the left leg to find his inner thigh and calf peppered with small shrapnel holes but only very minor bleeding. With no serious wounds to the left leg, I checked for a pulse in the left foot, and upon finding one I simply wrapped the entire leg with gauze. It was at that moment, I knew our boy was going to make it home.

About two years ago, I found myself struggling with the idea of a Soldier losing a limb or making the decision to apply a tourniquet to a severely bleeding arm or leg. I could not shake the idea of going through life with a missing extremity. I had approached our doctor about my insecurity and he simply told me this, "Josh, it's either their leg or their life. A mother would much rather see her child again." It was after this short but very powerful statement that I really knew the value of our quick decisions as medics to ensure everyone makes it home to their loved ones.

Behind me, the other two patients were being tended to by our other teams of medics. All three had the severe bleeding from their severed legs stopped, all had an IV flowing through each arm and, most importantly, all three were going to make it home to their loved ones.

A call came from one of the HMMWV ambulances, "Med-evac birds are five minutes out."

We finalized the bandaging on all three and loaded them into the back of our two awaiting ambulances for the two-minute drive to the landing pad to meet the incoming med evac helicopters. The race to meet the aircraft was successful and exactly ten minutes after loading the patients onto the ambulances, they were on their way to the combat support hospital.

The surge of adrenaline through our bodies kept the August heat far from our minds during the entire ordeal. The exhaustion began to creep up on us as we made our way back to the front gate to gather up the supplies we had left on the ground when we transported our patients to the med evac birds. We made our way around the front gate, all soaked in sweat, reassuring that no one else was injured and sorting out medical supplies. No one spoke. Silent glances and prayers told of what had just transpired. The feeling was surreal. Most importantly, the Saber Squadron Aid

Station was 88 and 0 with combat casualties; 88 came in alive, 88 left alive. It was, after all, *our watch*.

CHAPTER EIGHT

Boom!

The noise is absolutely deafening. Eyes go black, then a smoky haze covers one's field of vision. The sound wave throws the human body like a piece of paper in a hurricane. Confusion renders one stupid for moments that seem like precious hours. All of this came from the now infamous IED road-side bombs. The headlines were true, "In the town of Al Fallujah, it was not if, but when and how many troops would be hit by an IED."

***

The noon convoy rolls out of the front gates of our forward operating base in Al Habbaniyah towards the final destination, a compound in southern Fallujah forty-five minutes away. PFC Ricky Becktel drives the LMTV (Light Mobile Tactical Vehicle), a four-wheel truck the size of the more commonly recognized 2 1/2 ton vehicle. I stand through the hatch of the roof with my feet occupying the middle seat, Staff Sergeant Mike Schantz occupies the passenger seat pulling security from his side, and Specialist

Joe Brown sits in the canvas covered bed of the vehicle operating as rear security. Fifteen trucks form the snake of vehicles; ours in one of the middle positions: Lucky Number Seven.

The drive is simple, requiring only two turns and a few tight spots in the road. Still, as we keep our fifty-meter distance between vehicles, all eyes are alert and all weapons are ready - it is, after all, Fallujah.

I begin to play games in my head, much like I did on every convoy. *What if we get attacked from that house? What if he opens fire? Could I hit that guy on the roof from this distance in a moving vehicle?* It is my sick childhood G.I. Joe fantasy; it is the Game Seven, Bases Loaded, Bottom of the Ninth, Two Outs scenario where I'm down to my last magazine and the fate of everyone rests solely on me. I also sing Don McLean's "American Pie" (the six verse version) over and over in my head because after each completion of the song, another eleven minutes has passed. It keeps me sharp and keeps time moving. Plus it is one of the very few non-Garth Brooks songs that I know in its entirety.

My sharp eye sees nothing at the moment that I am half way through the song when all of a sudden the 'music died'. I am blown into the cab of the truck, unable to control the force of my body crumpling onto the seat. The blast feels like it ripped my body in two. My vision blurred, I reach behind my back, certain my hand would return soaked in blood. I then check the back of my legs, groin, and neck. No blood. The thunderclap leaves my ears echoing a dull thud as the outside world goes silent. "Holy shit!" I shout, "What the ...," I stop myself as I realize that, one, I can't hear myself shouting and two, we have just been hit by an IED.

Still squatting down in the cab, I shout to SSG Schantz, "I think that damned thing came up through the back of the truck.

I'm going to see if Joe Brown is okay." SSG Schantz responds, but all I can hear is a faint echo in my ears. I pop my head back through the roof hatch expecting to see the back canopy and cargo space blown to shreds. The rear of the vehicle is still intact, but there are shrapnel holes all throughout the canopy. I call for SPC Brown to give me a signal if he is okay, but he cannot hear over the engine and the lasting percussion of the blast.

I squat back down into the cab and shout to PFC Becktel, "You alright?" as he drove us out of the 'kill zone.' He pats my knee and shouts, "Hell, no. Where the hell did that come from?"

"I have no idea," I shout back.

"Dude, I can't hear a damn thing." I look over to SSG Schantz and repeated my last statement to him. "Hey," I shouted, "I'm going back up. If you need anything or need me to shoot something, tap my foot." He gives me the thumbs up. The entire chain of events from explosion to this point was a matter of mere seconds.

Once again I pop my head back through the roof. I tell myself that if it moves on the side of the road, I will kill it. There is no one. It is noon and the road and roadside are deserted. I once again call out to SPC Brown. Still no response; at least none that I am capable of hearing. I keep the muzzle of my M-16 assault rifle concentrated on the side of the road for the next mile until we stop for our security halt.

The circle intersection where we are stopped is probably not the best idea because of all the IED attacks in that exact spot in the past, but the convoy makes the halt there anyway. We disrupt movement of civilian traffic in all directions to prevent any other attacks and to keep cars from moving back into the 'kill zone' where vehicles are still trapped. In an instant, every muzzle is trained on any given car waiting for anyone to make the wrong move.

I look down to see if SSG Schantz knows how long we are going to be here. Without my knowing it, he has left the cab of the truck. "Ricky, where did Mike go?" He shrugs his shoulders back at me. *Where the hell did he go?*

At that moment a lieutenant hurriedly walks by the truck, counting the number of vehicles he has with him. "Hey sir," I shout "where did my T.C. (SSG Schantz) go?" He shouts back something I can't make out and continues walking to the rear of the line of vehicles. I keep my weapon focused on the Iraqi in the tractor in front of me as my eyes wander about searching for SSG Schantz. I can't figure out where he may have gone or what he is doing.

As the LT walks hurriedly back by the truck, again I call his attention, "Hey sir, have you seen Sergeant Schantz?"

Through his hand motions and what I can make out from reading his lips I hear, "He went back."

He went back? Back where? To the kill zone? Did he really run a mile back down the road to treat injuries? I didn't understand, but I am sure that wherever he went we will follow with the truck.

A few moments later, the lieutenant climbs into our truck, gives some instructions to PFC Becktel, and before I know it, we are following a Bradley fighting vehicle en route to the MEK. *Why are we not going back for SSG Schantz?*

The LT sits shotgun with his M-4 carbine concentrated out the window as PFC Becktel struggles to steer the truck and keep his bulkier M-16 focused out his window. The LT pulls out his sidearm M-9 Beretta and hands it over to PFC Becktel to make it easier in the event he should have to drive and shoot. PFC Becktel makes sure that everyone on the crowded main road sees he is armed and dangerous – he is pissed and wants the world to know it.

The three or four miles back to the MEK are consumed in my mind by a mass of confusion and the pain of the dull echo associated with my hearing loss.

When we reach the safety of the front gates, I duck in through the roof of the truck and sit on the seat that had been occupied by my feet the entire trip. The adrenaline is still coursing through my veins and I know it is only a matter of time before the after-effect headache sets in. The Bradley vehicle breaks formation and allows our LMTV to pull ahead of him to get to our destination inside the compound. Our speed increases as we follow the signs to C Med Company of the 82nd Airborne. The only reason I can think that we are here is to assist when SSG Schantz brings patients back from the 'kill zone.'

Our truck comes to a sudden stop in front of the building that houses the medical company, and this is where PFC Becktel and the LT make a quick exit from the cab and run to the rear of our vehicle. I clear my weapon and make my way to the pavement. What I see next I can't believe: SSG Schantz and PFC Becktel have SPC Brown's arms around their necks, helping him to support his weight on his right foot because a flow of blood is coming from his left foot. It all made obvious sense now: *SSG Schantz went back - to the back of the truck. SPC Brown was hit by a piece of the bomb.* Nothing like laying out all the pieces to finally solve the puzzle.

I watch as medics run from the building to assist Brown into the treatment room. There is so much activity, yet only a faint echo of noise. A second later I feel a tap on my shoulder. I turn to face the person, unaware of who it could possibly be.

"Hey man, you okay?" I made out from reading his lips.

"I'm sorry," I shook my head "I can't really hear anything. Where are they taking Brown?"

"He'll be alright," he assures me, "why don't you come with me."

"I'm good," I insist, "just take me to see Brown."

Again he tells me SPC Brown will be okay, and then grabs me by the arm and leads me into the aid station.

I am placed in a treatment room and immediately seen by a P.A. He puts me through the whole patient screening routine, including looking into my ears to ensure my tympanic membranes are still intact.

Upon the completion of the examination, he assures me that my ear drums sustained no permanent damage and, that like with any loud noise that disrupts your hearing, the sense would eventually return. I did not care. All I am concerned with is seeing Joe

Brown. The P.A. gives me a bunch of Motrin and, after making sure nothing else was wrong with me, releases me from his care.

I move down the hallway and see SSG Schantz standing in the doorway of the other treatment room.

"You okay, man?" he asks, noticeably shook up about what happened to SPC Brown.

"Yeah."

I look in the treatment room to see SPC Brown lying on the litter, the top of his foot split open and covered in blood. The doctors have the bleeding controlled and SPC Brown is already feeling the doping effects of the morphine. "Hey Fans, what'sup?" He slurs under the influence of the drugs.

"Not much J.B. How you doin'?"

He gave me a look that explained everything.

"Stay tough J.B., you'll be alright. I'll see you when you get out of surgery."

***

I leave the aid station to take a walk outside to clear my now ringing head. Across the street I run into SSG Schantz and PFC Becktel again. Still very upset about what happened to SPC Brown, SSG Schantz is taking his emotions out on one of the combat stress team members. I run up to him and throw my arm around him. "Let's take a walk," I said, leading him and PFC Becktel towards the LMTV that is now parked behind the aid station.

I had not yet really seen the extent of the damage to our truck directly after the attack. What I was about to observe within that vehicle explains just how divinely protected the four of us were. SPC Brown's spot in the bed of the truck could not have been more perfectly placed. The fact that only his foot sustained damage was astonishing. All around where his head and body were positioned when the blast went off were shrapnel holes in the canvas. Other holes were blown through the tailgate, destroying his aid bag, our medical chests and litters. Two holes were blown in the canvas inches on either side of where I was standing through the roof of the truck at the time of attack. A piece of shrapnel headed towards PFC Becktel was stopped by the battery box only a few feet behind him. And the piece of shrapnel that hit SPC Brown was lodged in a crack between the bed and the cab of the truck right behind SSG Schantz. That was miraculous. What was truly Divine Intervention was the news that this particular IED was daisy-chained to two other IED's that went off simultaneously, each one blowing up in between vehicles and spraying them with shrapnel rather than each vehicle taking the full brunt of the blast.

When we finished our damage inspection of the vehicle and had collected the chunks of shrapnel that had remained imbedded in the frame and body, we all seemed to calm down and accept the fact that if SPC Brown turned out to be okay with what happened, than we would all be okay.

SPC Brown was patched up, evacuated to Germany, and then to the U.S. He promptly grew sick of being away from is buddies in Iraq and made request after request to return to duty once his foot was healed. Mid-December, SPC Brown found himself back on a plane to Iraq and received his Purple Heart upon reuniting with our unit at Al Asad airbase.

CHAPTER NINE

We Should Have Brought Our Toothbrushes...

The desert was whipping by at an incredible rate as the UH-60 Blackhawk helicopter held an altitude of a mind-numbing fifteen feet above ground level. As we race along, only gaining altitude to clear power lines, I split my focus between the dunes out the window to my left and the signals of the crew chief in front of me. My aid bag sits stuffed between my legs as I try to make myself comfortable on the floor of the metal bird. Only thirty minutes before I had been in shorts and a t-shirt playing street hockey behind our hospital at Al Asad.

I am taking slap-shots at our make-shift hockey goal in preparation for the game start time of 1500. This is one of the many ways that we learned to make time pass. My teammates, Specialist Joshua Peters and Specialist Ian Weber, and I, have just finished setting up the plywood boards to create our enclosed rink and are waiting on our opponents who are in the hospital finishing up daily shifts. We are coming off of an embarrassing loss from the previous week, so we are especially ready for today's game. However, we are about to hear why the game is going to have to wait.

Staff Sergeant Mike Schantz comes running out of the hospital, "Hey, Josh, you need to tear down the rink. We have twenty causalities coming in from FOB Tiger."

"What the hell happened?" I ask, all of a sudden no longer interested in our revenge.

"A convoy coming back from FOB Tiger was hit. They're bringing birds here to fly out some medics to the ambush site."

With a make-no-mistake-about-it look I said, *"Mike, I will be on that bird."*

He gives me a nod and a smile. "Go get your stuff on and get the hell back up here."

In the ensuing sprint, I run down to the barracks across the street, passing other medics on their way up to the hospital. I tear into my room and throw my desert uniform on over my P.T. clothing, grab my aid bag, M-16, and body armor. On my way out I notice the barracks are deserted and there is a tremendous crowd gathering at the hospital. I take off in a dead run through the window laden corridor of the administration wing of the hospital towards the back doors where the Blackhawk helicopter waits with rotors spinning. I am met at the rear doors by our troop First Sergeant. "First Sergeant, I am getting on that bird, right?" It is more of a statement than a question. He nods and tells me to hurry up. I give him a smile, letting him know he will not regret it. I finish my run at the awaiting aircraft about 100 meters from the back of the hospital. I am greeted by two other medics; SPC Peters, Staff Sergeant Shay Black, and a PA. As my legs clear the ground and I slip into the back of the aircraft, the door slams shut behind me and we are airborne.

So many questions still fill my thoughts. We are not exactly sure how many patients we have on the ground. We don't know if the ambush firefight is still going on. All I know is we are hauling ass across the desert with the idea we are going to land in the middle of chaos.

We arrive at the ambush site thirty minutes after departure from Al Asad. The four of us lock and load our weapons and dismount the aircraft onto a two lane road surrounded on all sides by dunes of dry desert sand. Our eyes scan the dunes on either side in search of any enemy still present. Apache gun ships circle overhead of the two miles of road containing the stopped vehicles of the crippled convoy. The afternoon November air was very comfortable across my face as my feet carry my body and the weight of my aid bag across the pavement to the first vehicle.

"Where are the casualties?" I asked in unison with the others.

We are directed to a flat-bed LMTV (Light Military Tactical Vehicle) right behind the vehicle where we now stand. Our eyes move to the truck and our bodies follow as we run to assess the number of patients and their conditions. SPC Peters and the PA are the first to the truck and immediately hop up on the flat bed five and a half feet off the ground. SSG Black follows the both of them onto the back of the six-wheeler.

"Josh," I call up as they are beginning their patient assessment, "I'm better off down here. I'll prep IV bags and dressings. Just tell me what you need."

Blood begins to slosh over the edge of the truck bed.

"Kerlex," he shouts back, "lots and lots of kerlex."

SPC Peters discovers the gaping hole in one patient's face and knows there is an immediate need for the dressing. Because of the severe facial bleeding and trauma to the jaw, the patient's airway is also in jeopardy. I see him search his aid bag and locate his bulb syringe to suction the airway. This method will only work for so long; we know he has to get to that evacuation bird quickly.

I rip open my aid bag and reach instantly for the kerlex, large gauze bandages that I keep in good supply because they are so versatile; capable of being used on all sorts of wounds, and light; making them easy to pack. I throw four packages up at him and ask if he needs anything else.

"Fans," SSG Black calls for me from the left side of the truck, "help me get this guy down."

I give him a nod and instruct another Soldier to start prepping IV bags from my aid bag.

With the help of four Soldiers from the convoy, SSG Black and I gently roll one of the casualties off of the truck and place him on a cot they have set up beside the left rear tire. "Hey buddy," I spoke looking into the Soldiers' peaceful eyes, "how you doing?" He does not respond. "Shay, what's up?" I ask, puzzled.

"No pulse, no breathing."

"CPR?" I ask.

"No, the PA called it..." his voice trailed off. "He's gone."

A round had entered at the armpit of his left side with no exit wound: An open chest wound that has taken us forty-five minutes to get to.

For the first time as a medic, I feel mortally helpless. I want a chance for this Soldier! Everyone deserves a chance. Medics are the chance. I bow my head for a moment and I open my heart, "Lord..." It is my open-ended prayer that I reserve for fallen brothers and sisters on the battlefield. It is a prayer that I don't have the words for because it goes deeper than human thoughts allow. It opens me up to allow the groans of my prayer to be heard. I raise my head knowing that the Lord had brought our brother home and we have a task to save the other Soldier still on the truck. He still has a chance.

Quickly, SSG Black and I identify the KIA Soldier and wrap his body in a poncho for transport by helicopter to Mortuary Affairs. Then both of us turn our attention to the other Soldier lying on the blood-stained bed. I jump up to assist SPC Peters and Lt. Welch.

"Where do you need me?"

"At the head," Peters replies, "Hold C-spine."

"What's up, where's he hit?"

"The jaw," Peters indicates, "look at the left side of his face."

As I lower my head to see the damage, the patient lets out a gargled scream. The left side of his lower jaw is a mangled piece of bone and flesh. Peters is literally holding his face together the best he can. I cannot understand how he is still able to speak.

Over the next few minutes we work to clear all the blood and bone fragment from his airway, using mechanical suction provided by the bird and manual suction from the bulb syringe that Peters had in his aid bag. IV access is initiated to allow for a mainline for pain reducing drugs when he reaches the "Level Two" treatment facility. More gauze bandages are applied to reduce bleeding and provide support for the rest of what remains of his fragile jaw. Unbelievably, he can still speak when we require it of him to ensure the airway is still patent. He is not giving up and neither are we.

When the PA is satisfied with the treatment provided, we move the patient onto a litter and double-time to the awaiting med-evac bird. With adrenaline pumping, his 200 lb plus muscular frame is easy to lift. Our boy is going to live.

Still unsure as to how many casualties are involved with the convoy, the four of us work our way back to the LMTV and question the Soldiers who had helped with our treatments.

"That was it," came the response to our inquiry on the number of wounded.

"The message we received relayed multiple wounded and dead."

"The convoy was split during the ambush, we sent the message expecting the worst and hoping for the best."

That response caught me a little off guard.

Our PA, unsatisfied with not making sure everyone was okay personally (and rightfully so), asks us to walk to each vehicle checking on each crew member. Without hesitation, we start our walk down the line double and triple-checking everyone for any sort of injuries. Everyone assures us that they are fine, only a little shook up due to the recent ambush. A combat engineer accompanied us for additional security.

As we walk the line of vehicles, the Blackhawk helicopters that had taxied us out here took off and left the scene. The noise of the rotor blades is now replaced by a quiet dusk. Peters and I look at each other with the same thought in our minds. *How the hell are we getting back?*

"Sergeant Black, how the hell are we getting back?" I echo my thought out loud.

He and Peters seem just as puzzled as I am about our situation. Together, we walk over to the closest LMTV with MTS. "Do us a favor and contact Scalpel X-ray," Black asks the sergeant sitting in the passenger seat. "We need to find out how the hell we're getting home."

The E-5 in the cab agrees and types our request over the satellite instant message system. A moment later the response came back, 'The medic team will stay out with the convoy over night.' *Overnight. Damnit. And me without my toothbrush...*

"How long are we going to be here?" SSG Black asks our new source of information.

After typing the question into the MTS computer and waiting a minute for a response, the sergeant tells us, "They're fixing a couple of damaged trucks at the rear of the convoy. As soon as we get them rolling we'll be moving out to the dam."

The cold November night air begins to chill the sweat that has collected on my brown t-shirt during the treatment and evacuation of the two Soldiers. The four of us have only brought our aid bags and battle gear and have no cold weather gear. The trump card: I found out while walking the line that every bit of ammo has been expended during the ambush. My eight magazines, SSG Black's seven magazines, and Peters' six magazines were the only protection the twenty-five plus vehicle convoy now has. *Nice. We have no idea how long we're going to be stuck out here and we have just enough ammo to put up a five minute fight should anyone decide to launch another attack.*

Together, the four of us decide that should another attack happen while we are still stuck on this two lane road in the middle of the desert, we will be better off dividing up magazines then rather then now and risk losing our ammo should we really need it ourselves later. We are just a bit more comfortable with a full load of bullets.

The PA finds us leaning against a tire of a HMMWV swapping anecdotes about our current situation. "Did you hear we're here for the night?" I ask as she approaches while the last bit of light ducks below the horizon.

"No!?" she proclaims, both confused and yet unsurprised at the same time. Switching subjects she inquires, "Did you guys find anyone else needing treatment?"

We shake our heads 'no' insuring her again that we talked to each and every person. "Guess what else?" I add rhetorically,

"Specialist Peters, Sergeant Black and I are the only people here with ammo. Well, you have your M9 sidearm so we should be okay right?" I hope she reads the sarcasm in my voice.

There is nothing else to do but sit around and freeze...and wait. Hours are going by and our thoughts turn from our security, which seems by now to not be in any jeopardy, to our normal, 'back home' or 'remember when,' conversations. We search for remnants of MRE's in the back of a HMMWV. The cold is now every bit as miserable as the recent summer heat had been, and we finally concede to 'spoon' to stay warm, a huge step for Peters, given his ill feelings towards any kind of irregular contact. But it is cold, it is getting colder, and we have no cover. This is no time for pride. Our minds are miles away from the horror we have seen just hours before and now are dedicated to our own survival. Our only reminders of the mission that brought us to this state as we finally drift into a not-so-peaceful sleep are the blood-soaked knees of our DCUs (Desert Camouflage Uniform).

Our exhaustion has reached its absolute peak when we finally roll into the dam around 0300. The night has proved to be uneventful, yet stressful enough in our thoughts of another attack and the endurance of the bitter cold. It had not been our choice to remain with the convoy, but with all the scenarios that could have played out, I'm glad the four of us remained on scene. We were the medical response team. That two lane road in the middle of the sand was *our watch*.

CHAPTER TEN

Fallujah: Hell.

Dreamland. It is an oasis in the middle of hell; a four mile perimeter lake surrounded on all sides by palm trees and vacation villas, encompassed by twenty five foot walls to create a sanctuary for the Baath party on the south side of Al Fallujah. It is a taste of paradise superimposed onto the sand-ridden and war torn landscape of Iraq. It is home to Saber Squadron, 3rd Armored Cavalry Regiment from May of 2003 until the hand-over to the 3rd Infantry Division in mid July of the same year. The one hundred-twenty degree heat is made tolerable by the magnificent scenery of our lake resort.

A major operation is going down in the heart of the city. Just after midnight, the 101st Airborne Division, with support from Saber Squadron, is going after a high value target.

"We need FLA teams and the aid station up 100%," is the order given when the mission starts. We all lay on our cots in full DCUs, minus our boots, and slept lightly knowing the call will be coming. An eerie feeling pervades our thoughts and makes us believe medical support will be necessary. We sometimes hate being right.

The first call comes in a little after 0100. "Five wounded coming to your front gates on a non-standard."

"Let's move," came the order from the aid station NCOIC.

There is confusion about where they are bringing the casualties. Why are they going to the front gate and not to the aid station? We are much better equipped to handle the wounded in our lighted and fully equipped building. We have four treatment litters set up with ATLS (Advanced Trauma Life Support) sets at each station. Treating the patients at the gate takes away from our advantage of the system of treatment we have trained on for such a scenario. The PA argues the call, but there is no overturning the decision. We are going to have to treat out of our aid bags and FLAs on the sand at the pitch dark perimeter gate.

Ten medics and two PAs board the two FLAs and we take off towards our rendezvous point. I drive the first HMMWV and make the five minute trip in about half the time, nearly rolling the vehicle because I am taking the corners at such a high rate of speed. There are no short-cuts because the narrow road skirts the entire lake. Fast is the only way to make up on time to ensure we beat the non-standard evac vehicle to the gates. I drive as fast as the wheels will turn.

In a cloud of dust stirred up by the loose sand, I bring the FLA to a stop in a clearing about 100 meters inside the front gates. The night is so dark that at first we don't even see the Blackhawk helicopter waiting only a couple vehicle distances away from our position. Our treatment area is not ideal, but at least we have the med-evac bird ready to lift off as soon as we treat the wounds.

Five minutes behind us comes the second FLA and with it, the rest of the team. We pull our eight litters out and place them on the ground, readying them for the incoming wounded. Seconds later, headlights come tearing around the corner and break the darkness of our sand box. Two HMMWVs and an LMTV halt to the left of the litters. Screams of pain come from the bed of the large LMTV as the tailgate is dropped to allow us access. We immediately begin our work to unload the patients from the truck to the ground five feet below. The task takes only minutes as we bring the bloody Soldiers to the awaiting litters. Two medics per patient, we work diligently to stop bleeding from gunshot wounds, splint fractured limbs, and start IV lines. The scene is a mess made worse by the gathering crowd of spectators. As we treat, we continuously yell to keep people back because their interest in the events only hinders our ability to move around freely to gather supplies, as well as blocks our only source of light from the headlamps of the vehicles. Eventually they get the message and clear a big enough area to allow for our elbow room.

I am on a constant route from the patients to the FLAs to bring oxygen, suction, and extra medical supplies from the chests on the roof of the vehicle. I stop at each patient only for a moment to allow for the two other medics to request additional supplies. A gunshot wound to the arm, two head injuries, and two gunshot wounds to the legs make up the motley list of injuries. Blood soaks the clothing of the four men who lay in our care. No more than ten to fifteen minutes after touching our first patient we are ready to load the awaiting helicopter.

The loading process is rough. The darkness and the terrain make for a challenge in negotiating each litter to the patient berths inside the bird. Once to full capacity, the chopper takes off en route to the CSH. The twelve of us make our way back to the FLAs where we are met by our fifth patient, a Soldier with a 'through and through' gunshot wound to his right upper leg. His mood is the strangest I have ever seen for a person who has been shot. In a very nonchalant way he walks to the edge of the truck, drops his pants and shows us the entrance and exit wounds to his thigh.

"I guess I got shot," he says, shrugging his shoulders. "It hurts like hell but I think I'll be okay."

We have the other FLA drive him back to the aid station to clean his wound and take precautions to make sure the non life-threatening wound was just that. Meanwhile, the PA, two other Saber medics and I stay at the site to wait for the one Soldier who was killed during the firefight. We decide to package the body here rather than the aid station so as not to expose the body to the patient at the aid station.

After waiting about ten minutes and having no vehicle show, we call over the radio to get a status on the situation. Again a decision has been made for us and the body was driven to the aid station after all. The PA grows frustrated for the lack of respect for his orders, but again has to concede to the new situation.

We arrive at the aid station to find a cargo HMMWV parked in the grass in front of the building. Blood not only fills the rear cargo area, but also spills droplets on the ground. The Soldier's body has been taken to the abandoned structure beside our treatment building where it lay under a poncho awaiting identification. The PA moves inside the building and with the Soldiers' squad leader and platoon leader, makes positive identification of the body, removes personal items, positions the body to a restful position, and recites a short prayer.

I move inside the aid station where I continue treatment with the Soldier who has the through and through gunshot wound. As I irrigate the wound with a saline solution he tells me that the Soldier who was killed was hit by an RPG in the chest. "The strange thing," he tells me, "was that he and I had just switched seats in the back of the HMMWV just before he was killed." The unbelievable luck that this Soldier escaped with only a gunshot wound strikes me hard. "It should have been me," he says with the same nonchalant tone as before.

I continue to clean the hole, not knowing how to respond. When the PA is satisfied with the cleanliness of the wound, I look the Soldier in the eye and tell him the only thing I can think of with such a heavy chain of events weighing on his mind; "Take it easy and get some rest."

The rest of the night is spent re-fitting our supplies and cleaning out the HMMWV. We each take our own way of paying our respects to our fallen brother. The squad leader and platoon leader each sleep against the outside wall of the building, refusing to leave their Soldier's side until he is taken out by helicopter the next morning.

The dawn breaks a few hours later and the PA and I help load the litter bearing the body of the Soldier onto the FLA for the drive to the LZ. His squad leader and platoon leader sit in the back maintaining their constant vigil. As always, the drive is hot and dusty, but this particular drive has the somberness of a funeral procession. Out of respect, I do not want to drive too fast. Upon reaching the Blackhawk, the four of us carry the litter the last 50 meters to the patient berth. The black body bag is covered in a thin layer of dust from the drive. Before loading the body, the two 101st Soldiers place their hands on the bag, leaving their handprints as a last show of respect and love for their fallen brother. Tears in their eyes, they turn away and walk back to the war. They have a watch to continue. They know the fallen would understand.

CHAPTER THIRTEEN

Now Where Did That Patient Go?

I love sleeping. I hate not sleeping. I hate being awakened in the middle of the night. I love my job. Sometimes my job wakes me in the middle of the night. So, I love not sleeping if it means a job has to be done. It's a vicious cycle!

"Hey Fans, we've got an accident south of Ramadi."

I knocked the sleep out of my eyes and asked how many patients.

"Don't know. You'll be rolling out with QRF (Quick Reaction Force) in about ten minutes. You good?"

"Yeah, wake up Brown and Becktel," I said putting on my boots.

It was hot. It was dark and hot.

Our HMMWV rolled out the front gates with an escort QRF vehicle en route to the crash site, PFC Becktel driving, SPC Joe

73

Brown in the passenger seat, and I was in the back of the ambulance prepping splints and IV bags.

"Ricky, J.B.," I called up through the bulkhead doors, "I want to have these guys packaged up and back in the ambulance in twenty minutes. I want to spend no more than twenty minutes on the ground. When we get there we're going to split up and triage. Tell me what you've got and we'll work from there. You got it?"

They both responded with a yes and confirmed what I had just instructed.

The accident was on the side of a highway dubbed 'RPG (Rocket Propelled Grenade) Alley' from all of the caches of weapons and attacks mounted from the stretch of road. PFC Becktel drove about 50 meters off the road onto a bumpy dirt shoulder.

I jumped out of the rear doors onto a mound of dirt that caught me by surprise because I only fell about two feet. *Stupid terrain.* The three of us sprinted over to a four-seater HMMWV that was resting on its underbelly with all four tires trapped in two parallel ditches. Right behind the quadriplegic vehicle was a Bradley fighting vehicle.

"Where are the patients?" I asked to the first person I saw at the crash site.

"We've got one over there, two over there, and the fourth is over...I don't know where the fourth is."

"I don't know where the fourth is". What the hell kind of person lets injured people get away from him? And why the hell are they so spread out? I didn't have time to give a lecture on patient care or accountability.

"Ricky, check those guys out," I said pointing to the two Soldiers laying twenty-five feet away. He gave me a nod and hurried to tend to his patients.

"J.B., go see what's up with that guy over there," I said motioning to the other Soldier laying the same distance away on the other side of the HMMWV.

"I'm going to find our wayward patient," I said with a noticeable sigh of frustration.

When I found the fourth wounded Soldier, he was in the back of another HMMWV about twenty meters over rough terrain away from the wrecked vehicle. Sitting upright, he had a cloth to his profusely bleeding forehead. *Great, this guy just walked twenty meters with a head/neck injury.* I climbed into the back of the truck with him and saw the gash that exposed his skull over his left eye.

"Hey sergeant, how's it going?" I said grabbing either side of his head at the ears to stabilize his head and spine. "Looks like you've got a pretty nice cut there. Without moving can you tell me what happened?"

Through broken English intermixed with gibberish he recounted the accident telling me he got knocked around in the turret of the Bradley.

"Alright, I need to put this C-collar around your neck. It's going to keep your spine inline. Okay?"

"No," he said in a very confused hushed tone.

Damn this guy is messed up. "Hey sergeant, I'm just gonna put this C-collar around your neck," I said again as if I were saying it to him for the first time.

"Okay," he agreed in the same confused hushed tone.

It was like dealing with a child: The more convincing I sounded, the more he cooperated.

I then tended to his wound in the same manner. When I was finished bandaging, I instructed another Soldier to keep him talking and to absolutely not let him move for fear of paralysis while I went for a spine board and a litter. He assured me he'd follow my instruction and I took off for the ambulance.

On my way back to the vehicle, I ran into PFC Becktel. "What's up?" I asked.

"Possible fractured tib-fib on one and a possible fractured right arm or dislocated right shoulder on the other."

"C-collars?"

"Yes."

"Splinted?" I asked hoping for a yes.

"Yeah, one of the guys already had the leg splinted when I got to him."

"What about the shoulder?"

"Splinted."

"Sling?"

"Not yet."

Damnit. "Alright, do me a favor; I'll work on these guys, I need you to stabilize the staff sergeant on the back of the truck onto a short-board and a litter. I want him elevated from the waist up. Put blankets between the spine board and the litter to do that. Understood?"

He gave me a nod and took off to execute the order.

What I saw next immediately pissed me off. On the lower leg that had been "splinted" was the worst attempt at immobilization I had ever seen. One piece of splinting material about eight inches long held on by two zip-ties was some fog-brain's idea of a proper splint. *Only twenty minutes on the ground...right...that was wishful thinking!*

I vented my frustration on the nearest person, "Who the hell splinted this?"

"One of the CLS guys," he responded.

"He's fired," I shot back.

I cut off the hindrance and applied a proper immobilizing splint, checked the distal pulse and told the Soldier I'd be right back.

"So your arm hurts," I joked to the next patient in obvious pain from his injured extremity. "We'll you're in good hands." Two cravat cloth bandages and a few ties later, I had his injured arm in a sling and swathe. Once completed, I directed four of the closest Soldiers to immobilize the two patients onto spine boards, ensuring they did not cause further injury to their wounds or spines.

Running back over to PFC Becktel, I saw him completing the task of securing the head injury patient to the litter in the fashion

I had directed. I double checked his work, which proved to be all that I had asked of him and more, then told him to go help SPC Brown work on the pelvic fracture. "I'll be right behind you," I added.

Sweat was pouring from my face when I made it over to SPC Brown and PFC Becktel working on the fourth patient who was lying on his back with his knees flexed in obvious pain from his current situation. "Talk to me, boys, what's up?"

"Possible pelvic fracture." SPC Brown remarked in his perfect, 'by the book voice.'

"Blankets," I directed to the nearest bystander, "go to the FLA and grab me three green blankets."

"What am I thinking?" I asked, testing my two medics.

"Support." PFC Becktel snapped off in perfect sync with my question.

"What do you think J.B.?" I asked in response to PFC Becktel's answer.

He nodded his head in uncertain agreement, frustrated in the amount of time he'd already spent working on the patient. We could afford no more time on site. It was time to get moving and I had to hurry us up.

The blankets came seconds after my request. I snatched them and began to pack them between the Soldiers flexed knees and the spine board on which he rested. Another blanket I cut to wrap around his injured hips to provide additional support. Once I was satisfied with the packaging I directed PFC Becktel and SPC Brown to "Wrap tape around everything. I do not want him to be able to move an inch."

I took the next few moments to re-triage our four injured Soldiers and to appoint litter teams to load the FLA. With a stress in my voice indicating that we'd been on scene way too long, I hurried everyone along in the loading process. Upon completion, PFC Becktel and I shut the rear doors securing SPC Brown and the four patients in the back and fired up the truck to start our drive back to the awaiting aid station.

I was pissed. I was told we were being dispatched to pick up four patients already packaged and ready for loading. Not that I minded the task we had just completed, but we had a serious communication breakdown from the accident scene to our dispatch. Our being gone for over an hour made my team look bad in the eyes of the doctor and medics waiting at the Ramadi aid station.

My frustration was vented when we finally reached the gutted building that housed our treatment area. I demanded to know why I was told medics were already on the scene and had the patients ready for our pick up when, in actuality, we had to Easter-egg hunt our wounded. Granted, the three of us performed to a higher standard, but misinformation can lead to confusion and mission failure.

Our fault in the matter was cleared upon my recount of events on scene and we were praised for our proficiency and professionalism in treating the four injured Soldiers. Later in the evening, as dawn began to break over the city, we loaded the four men onto med-evac birds for evacuation to a higher echelon of care. Updates of their injuries a few days later indicated that our treatment was timely and exact to control the wounds present and proper in preventing any further complications.

We learned to adapt to misinformation and perform to a higher standard. It was our watch and our duty to our brothers.

Lullabies

They fall every night about an hour after the evening prayer. Some nights they are distant booms and others they shake the buildings. The explosives land everywhere. Everyone has a story about the mortar that hit too close. They are our mortar lullabies: After they fall we can go to sleep. It is weird to say that one can get used to such a frightening thing, but war is stupid that way.

PICTURES

SPC Peters and SGT Taylor pose for a picture at Al Asad airbase.

SPC Fansler re-enlists for Ft. Carson, Colorado at Kandihar
Airport, Kandihar, Afghanistan.

SPC Peters provides driver's side security in Support Squadron Commander's vehicle en route to FOB Tiger for 'Operation Rifles Blitz'.

The mountains to the west of Fire Base Lwara. Lwara, Afghanistan.

Left to right. SPC Peters, SGT Ruth and SSG Pagan prepare to depart FOB Byers in their FLA (Forward Line Ambulance).

SPC Fansler stands in front of seized weapons during a cordon
and search of a small village in Afghanistan.

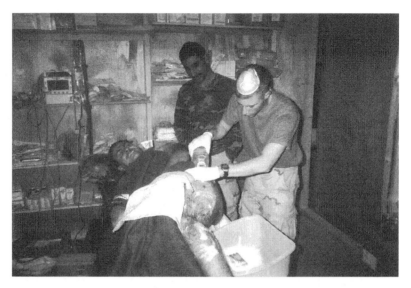

SPC Peters treats a Coalition Soldier with shrapnel wounds received during 'Operation Rifles Blitz'.

A 571st Medical Company (Air Ambulance) helicopter approaches to transfer patients to Al Asad airbase.

Left to right. PFC Becktel, SPC Nunez, SPC Campos and SPC Brown pass the time at 'TAA Rifles' with a game of Spades.

Med Troop Soldiers prepare their HMMWV ambulances at 'TAA Rifles' for the move north to Al Asad airbase.

SPC Fansler rides a camel in Organ-E Fire Base, Organ-E, Afghanistan.

SPC Peters pulls security near his FLA while their convoy stops en route to FOB Byers.

SPC Fansler at the entrance to Fire Base Lwara. Lwara, Afghanistan.

SPC Peters pauses for a picture while performing last minute checks on his FLA before departure to FOB Tiger.

SPC Fansler at FOB Salerno, Afghanistan.

Left to right. SGT Hardy, PFC Sheehan, SPC Peters, and SPC Campos before night duty at First Squadron's aid station.

Med Troop's M113-A3 track ambulances stand ready for duty at Al Asad airbase.

SPC Fansler conducts cordon and search in remote Afghan
village, September 2002.

Road sign providing a choice for the lesser of the two evils: Al
Ramadi or Al Hit-Haditha.

Land mines and bandoliers confiscated by Coalition forces and set for destruction.

Boxes full of land mines discovered by EOD (Explosive Ordinance Disposal).

Laundry day in Afghanistan.

---SECTION TWO---
By: Joshua M. Peters

INTRODUCTION

Lest We Forget...

Those who profess to favor freedom, and yet depreciate agitation, are men who want rain without thunder and lightning.

--Frederick Douglass

As I worked and studied my way through college at Taylor University I struggled with the same question most every young man and woman wrestles with at this age. "What am I going to do after I graduate?" This rural Indiana college had plenty to offer; I should know, I changed majors three times. I finally decided in my Sophomore year that I wanted to work with troubled youth. I had always related well with children and I desired a profession that would make me feel like I was making a difference in somebody's life. Upon completing my internship of summer camp counseling and directing in Ireland the summer after my Junior year, I returned to campus for my Senior year, to complete my preparation for the "real world."

Even though I was certain about my future career decision, the idea of military service also continued to appeal to me. I often thought about my grandfathers and my father's uncle who served in WWII. More than one Purple Heart lay among their treasured possessions. My mental list continued down the generations as I counted my father's brother who served as a Drill Instructor and as a member of the military police in the Air Force. I was proud to include my cousin who served with the Marines in Cuba and Haiti.

Pride in freedom and duty to country was an ideal with which I had been raised. I was beginning my Senior year in college and yet, the desire to serve in the military at times still weighed so heavily on my mind that I could clearly see the mental scale ever so slightly teetering, as if awaiting the circumstances that would tip the balance.

On this routine college morning, just as Summer is lobbing the football to Autumn, I once again begin tossing the idea of military service around in my head as I drive back to my apartment from breakfast. Deciding this is heavy subject matter for such a beautiful, sunny day, I turn on the radio in hopes of replacing the silence with a favorite tune. Nothing is on but news, news and more news. "Doesn't anyone play music anymore?" I think out loud to myself. I realize I am running late for class as I glance at my watch, it reads 8:53 AM. The date is September 11, 2001. Eight minutes ago, my world changed forever and I didn't even know it.

Without listening to what the newscasters have to say, I flip off the radio with a bit of disgust, park my car, and walk inside my apartment. The pale, white face of my roommate and his girlfriend speak volumes.

"Did you see this?" he says, his voice quivering.

I can tell by the look on his face it isn't good. I shake my head 'no' and peer past him at the TV. One tower stands smoking.

"Oh my God, what happened?" I ask. No one says anything. At this time it is still believed to be faulty piloting; early enough yet in those last remaining moments before unsuspecting innocence perished in our land; when to think otherwise is still incomprehensible.

I stand numbly watching the television, thinking about my relatives in New York. I try to call them to get more information. *Busy signal.* Just at that precise moment I see a second plane tear through the remaining tower. "What the hell is going on?" I ask no one in particular. Seconds are suspended in time and minutes pass like days as the media scramble for an explanation.

We all sit there, too numb to realize we are missing classes, glued to the television all day. I watch as the first tower fell, and am overcome with grief, when, unbelievably the second also gives way. The peaceful cocoon I had inhabited up until now has given me no frame of reference from which to comprehend all the death that has just taken place before my very eyes. Finally, the news begins dropping names: Osama bin Laden, Saddam Hussein, Hammas.

Just after 10:00 AM we hear that the passengers of United Airlines Flight 93 have all perished in a field in Shanksville, Pennsylvania. Upon hearing "Pennsylvania," it then occurs to me that my mother is directing a tour in that region right at that very moment. Tears begin to well in my eyes. I try to call her - busy signal. I call her company - busy signal. I dial and dial her work while the tears begin to fall from my eyes. I know nothing and become more frightened for her safety by the minute. I finally reach a clear line locally and I speak with my mother's friend at work.

"Joshua, relax," she says, not convincing me because of the obvious tears in her own voice. "Where is my mother?" I shout into the phone. "We are trying to reach her as soon as we can. All of the phones are either busy or down right now. I...don't... just pray." Her voice trails off. I hang up the phone.

I brace myself against the wall. I feel stupid for worrying over my mother when so many mothers, fathers, sons, and daughters were just murdered right before my eyes. I begin to do what my father taught me to do when I am in a tight spot. Pray.

"Dear God, be with all of the families of those killed and wounded today. Give them a peace that comes only from You. I don't know what is going on right now but You do, please help me understand. Please protect my family. Amen"

As I open my eyes, I realize a feeling welling up within me that shouldn't be there after praying. It is hate. I hate whoever it is for doing what they have just done. I hate them for taking away so many innocent lives and leaving the rest of America feeling so lost. I promise myself right then and there, I will dedicate the next few years of my life doing whatever I can to bring to justice those who hate freedom. In whatever small way I can, I resolve that I will protect our country from experiencing any more suffering of this kind. I am a young man, just like my relatives before me when they answered the call. It is now my heartfelt duty to serve my country and go to whatever corner of the earth these bastards are hiding in. I would finish my degree and enlist in the United States Army as a Combat Medic just three weeks after graduation. I determine in my heart that I will provide combat medicine to all Soldiers in need. With everything that is within me, I am compelled to abate the suffering of any Soldier under my care, reclaiming them from death's door, refusing to allow the enemy to count them among their victories, not on *my watch*.

***

"On Tuesday morning, September 11, 2001, terrorists attacked America in a series of despicable acts of war. They hijacked four passenger jets, crashed two of them into the World Trade Center's twin towers, a third into the Headquarters of the U.S. Department of Defense at the Pentagon, causing great loss of life and tremendous damage. The fourth plane crashed in the Pennsylvania countryside, killing all on board but falling well short of its intended target apparently because of the heroic efforts of passengers on board.

This carnage, which was caused by the collapse of both Trade Center towers and the destruction of part of the Pentagon, killed more than 250 airplane passengers and thousands more on the ground. Civilized people around the world denounce the evildoers who devised and executed these terrible attacks. Justice demands that those who helped or harbored the terrorists be punished -- and punished severely. The enormity of their evil demands it. We will use all the resources of the United States and our cooperating friends and allies to pursue those responsible for this evil, until justice is done.

We mourn with those who have suffered great and disastrous loss. All our hearts have been seared by the sudden and senseless taking of innocent lives. We pray for healing and for the strength to serve and encourage one another in hope and faith. Scripture says: "Blessed are those who mourn, for they shall be comforted."

I call on every American family and the family of America to observe a National Day of Prayer and Remembrance, honoring the memory of the thousands of victims of these brutal attacks and comforting those who lost loved ones. We will persevere through this national tragedy and personal loss. In time, we will find healing and recovery; and, in the face of all this evil, we remain strong and united, "one Nation under God."

NOW, THEREFORE, I, GEORGE W. BUSH, President of the United States of

America, by virtue of the authority vested in me by the Constitution and laws of the United States do hereby proclaim Friday, September 14, 2001, as a National Day of Prayer and Remembrance for the Victims of Terrorist Attacks on September 11, 2001. I ask that the people of the United States and places of worship mark this National Day of Prayer and Remembrance with noontime memorial services, the ringing of bells at that hour, and evening candlelight remembrance vigils. I encourage employers to permit their workers time off during the lunch hour to attend the noontime services to pray for our land. I invite the people of the world who share our grief to join us in these solemn observances.

IN WITNESS WHEREOF, I have hereunto set my hand this thirteenth day of September, in the year of our Lord two thousand one, and of the Independence of the United States of America the two hundred and twenty-sixth."

--PRESIDENT GEORGE W. BUSH

CHAPTER ONE

Brave Rifles!

You have been baptized in fire and have come out steel!

--Third Armored Calvary Regiment motto

When I arrive at Fort Carson, Colorado one question fills my head. *What was the real Army like?* I had been at basic training at Fort Leonard Wood, Missouri for nine weeks and then went straight to my medical school for four months at Fort Sam Houston in San Antonio, Texas. I have known nothing but basic training soldiering and combat medicine for the last seven months of my life. I am excited and yet apprehensive. I am not as confident in my skills as I want to be. I studied hard at Fort Sam and performed all of the required tasks to standard. In fact, I graduated twenty-second in a class of about three hundred. But just as my instructors said, anyone can pass a test with fake wounds and a grade sheet. I would come to find out that the real test would be when I found myself up to my elbows in American blood while the enemy sought to destroy us all.

Deployment is on my mind when I report for duty at Fort Carson in February of 2003. There are many rumors about where the deployment will take me; the only certainty is we are going somewhere. Turns out that "somewhere" would be to the Al Anbar providence in Iraq. This was the largest area of responsibility given to any one unit during the entire first year of conflict. This area also includes the very volatile "Sunni Triangle". The towns of Ar Ramadi, Al Fallujah, Al Qa'im, Al Baghdadi, Al Hit-Haditha, and Ar Rutbah would become very familiar to me. I am assigned to Ambulance Platoon, Medical Troop, Support Squadron, Third Armored Cavalry Regiment, known as "The Brave Rifles."

My first day in the unit my squad leader, Staff Sergeant Shay Black, takes me out for lunch. As we sit there enjoying our food and discussing various interests and apprehensions of mine, I can tell there is something he is eventually going to tell me. He waits for me to take a bite and slides a piece of paper across the table to me. My eyes fall on the heading and the first few words.

"3rd Armored Cavalry Regiment, Fort Carson, Colorado: To deploy to the CENTCOM area of responsibility: Kuwait..." The rest of the letter is inconsequential. This is it. At 22 years old, fresh out of training, I am going to war. I thought I was prepared for this, but the sinking feeling in my stomach tells me otherwise. The war in Iraq has now become a reality to me. Many more questions fill my mind; too many to even begin asking. He then tells me not to unpack very many of my things because we would be leaving within a month. Our vehicles have already been loaded onto a ship for transportation.

SSG Black informs me I am to be the driver of his M113-A3 Tracked Ambulance. I have seen plenty of pictures of the 113, but

I had never seen one in person. Since all vehicles were gone, I wondered when I would learn to drive this vehicle that I am to take into combat.

He answered audibly to my silent question: "The vehicles aren't here so we'll teach you to drive in Kuwait before we head north." Not exactly the response I am hoping for.

I take the next few weeks preparing myself and my family for what is certain to be tough times ahead. It is hard to admit it, but for the first time in my life, I am afraid. I am afraid of what I might encounter, I am afraid of leaving my family, and I am afraid of dying. I spend many hours talking to my parents and my brother about my deployment. I hide my fear from them the best I can. The last conversation that I had with my parents was very difficult for them. I instruct my brother to take care of my parents and to give them any help that they might need in the weeks and months ahead. I promise them I will be careful. I promise them that I would always follow their advice and look to God for answers when everything seems impossible. Little did I know just how impossible the next year was going to seem. I don't know exactly where I am going and I don't know for how long. I am still brand new to the unit; I don't have any friends in the unit to rely on. I don't like this feeling. The Soldier who was to become my extremely close friend and co-author of this book, Josh Fansler, hadn't yet reported to my unit from the 82nd Airborne Division. I was alone.

As if leaving family isn't difficult enough, I was presented with a personal blessing just a few weeks prior. I had met a young lady named Layla Price. A mutual friend of ours had tried to "set us up" many times before, but because of college and then my enlistment in the military, it had never worked out. Finally, we were able to meet during the week I was home before reporting to Fort Carson. I am completely smitten with her. Her contagious laugh and beautiful smile are captivating. We spent every single day that I was home together. Every second that we spent together was bitter-sweet. I was scared to leave such a wonderful woman behind when everything about her and me together was suddenly so perfect. She even came out to Colorado to visit me before I deployed. When she returned to Indiana, we were forced to say our good-byes with our future very uncertain.

As I board the plane on 01 April 2003 I am entering into a whole new phase of my life. Compared to the tasks that we all were about to undertake, everything in my life up to this point had been simple. I used to think high school was difficult, until I got to college. Then, college seemed like the hardest milestone of my life. Now here I am, making my way up the steps of a plane that is to carry me over 7,000 miles away to a very unfriendly land. For the first time in my life, I am faced with a situation that I have no control over. I felt proud that I could deploy overseas in defense of freedom, just like so many of my relatives before me have done. I have learned how to be a Soldier. I have learned how to be a Combat Medic. Now it is time for me to learn the importance of caring for other Soldiers on the battlefield. It is now *my watch*.

CHAPTER TWO

My First Encounter With Death

The good, the bad, hardship, joy, tragedy, love, and happiness are all interwoven into one indescribable whole that one calls life. You cannot separate the good from the bad, and perhaps there is no need to do so.

--Jacqueline Bouvier Kennedy Onassis

01 June 2003

Many people remember verbatim their "firsts". Where they were when they first learned to ride a bike. What the girl or boy's name was with whom they shared their first kiss. Or even what inspired them to say "I love you" for the first time.

Those "first" memories of mine have been joined with a new category since the deployment. My first encounter with death.

It is a typical night in the hospital at Al Asad. We are all still fairly new to the area, so much cleaning still needed to be done in order for the hospital to be brought up to the standard that is

107

required to fully treat patients. On this particular night when we are nearly finished cleaning for the day I decide to walk outside to enjoy a quick break. The stars are in abundance and the moon seems to smile at me. All seems well, except I notice one ambulance is missing. We usually keep two 113 tracked ambulances next to the hospital; only one is present. *Odd.*

Before I have too much time to contemplate the location of this vehicle, the unmistakable rumbling of the track makes its way to my ears. The ambulance veers sharply around the back of the hospital and makes an abrupt stop at the emergency room loading area. I run to see what is going on.

There is a crowd of doctors, medics and litter bearers already congregated at the back door. *I guess I am the last to know.* As the rear ramp drops to expose the ambulance's content, I hold my breath.

A sergeant runs past me and peers into the back. He turns around and shakes his head. "He's gone".

The sound of Specialist Joe Brown providing this patient with CPR is loud and unmistakable. "One, two, three, four, five....." I take a few steps closer to get a look at the patient. It is then the smell hits my face like a baseball bat. The smell is likened to a lighter's flame that singes hair coupled with the rotten odor of feces. My eyes begin to tear up and I choke down the vomit. Nothing could ever prepare me for what I was about to see.

This is an Iraqi man who had been attempting to steal weapons from a cache. When Soldiers tried to stop him, a gun battle ensued. It is obvious who the victor was.

This man was shot in the mandibular jaw, leaving most of his lower face hanging by a few pieces of flesh. This made CPR difficult since the BVM (Bag Valve Mask) is the only thing holding his face together. With every pushed bit of air SPC Brown attempts to pump into this man, bubbled blood oozes from a crack in his skull.

There is an entry bullet wound mid-axillary, right below the armpit. There is no exit wound. It is my guess that the bullet entered his chest cavity and bounced around a few times, severing every life sustaining organ.

The final wound is most certainly the main cause of the putrid smell. From the bottom of his feet up to his waist he was hit with a white phosphorous grenade. The chemical had dissolved all of the flesh and muscle on his legs, leaving them a ghostly white color. Quite a contrast from the dark olive color the rest of his body portrays. The skin around his knees is beginning to flake off like dandruff. This man appears to be half plastic, no need for medical attention.

As they carry the man inside the hospital to be officially declared dead by a medical doctor, I catch a glimpse of the man's face. *Death.* There is nothing like it. At the time, there was nothing like it to me in the universe. When life has left a man's body the look is unmistakable. His body is an empty shell that once housed a soul. A soul in this case that had every evil intention on gathering weapons with which to maim and kill American Soldiers.

This first experience with death due to combat will always be with me. It brought reality to the war that waged outside the perimeter of Al Asad. I knew then it was going to be a long and difficult tour. The smell and disgust of death would be something that I could never overcome and certainly never forget. My first encounter with death became something that would drive me to serve the Soldiers who would need me *on my watch*.

CHAPTER THREE

Trial by Fire

Four freedoms: The first is freedom of speech and expression - everywhere in the world. The second is freedom of everyone to worship God in his own way, everywhere in the world. The third is freedom from want . . . everywhere in the world. The fourth is freedom from fear . . . anywhere in the world.

--Franklin D. Roosevelt

13 June 2003

Although I had arrived in country in April, by mid-June I am still trying to acclimate to the heat of days that brought the temperatures well up to 120 degrees or higher. MRE's (Meals Ready to Eat) and sun baked water is our sustenance. I have only been in Iraq for two months and am trying to do my best to adapt to the environment of a war zone.

As of yet, I have not seen actual combat. I always wondered what it would be like, if it is really as bad as I have heard from my relatives. As a boy I saw John Wayne ascend the deadly hills of Iwo Jima many times. I have lost track of how many times I cheered on Tom Hanks as he stormed the beaches of France. But this is not Hollywood, there is no memorized script, and the Soldiers who die on this set don't get to enjoy their mocha lattes at the end of the day.

I had graduated from my combat medic school only four months before and am anxious to "do my part" in this war. I know the material. I strived to do my very best in my school because I knew it would be useful soon. While some spent the weekends drinking, I was perusing my notes. Others went to bed early; I went over various scenarios in my head until the early morning hours. September 11, 2001 was still fresh in all of our minds when I was at Fort Sam Houston during the fall and winter of 2002. Upon graduation, deployments were inevitable. At the time, my classmates and I figured deployment to Afghanistan for six months would be our lot, not once considering we would find ourselves in Iraq for a year.

I am curious about how I will handle myself under the pressure of a real life trauma. I have heard countless stories of medics who possessed all of the book knowledge but when it came time to put their knowledge into action, they froze and someone paid the ultimate price. I do not want to be that medic. Many curiosities and apprehensions fill my head. In the coming weeks and months, my questions would all soon be answered.

Our Squadron is based out of Al Asad, about ninety miles west of Baghdad. Belonging to the Ambulance platoon, it is our duty to pull what we call "first-up". This duty calls for us to sleep, eat, wash clothes, and basically live next to the hospital that our troop has cleaned out and set up. The building was once a hospital to the Iraqi military that served there. Early in our deployment, our evacuation vehicles are the solid but sluggish M113-A3 tracked ambulances. They have the armor that the HMMWV ambulances lacked. The downside is that the vehicle's top speed is somewhere between 30 and 40 miles per hour. Not the vehicle of choice if things took a turn for the worse and one needed to leave town in a hurry.

As I write letters home to my girlfriend and family I notice myself really missing home. I am still fairly new to the unit and am struggling to find my niche. I am contemplating the wild journey I have experienced in the last twelve months. I have traveled from the safety of the classrooms of rural Taylor University, through the rigors of basic training, spent months immersed in medical books and scenarios, and finally arrived in the barren and dangerous sands of Iraq. I am already thinking about going back home, not the best of ideas so early in the deployment, but it makes me happy to contemplate it. September will be here before we know it and our six month tour will be completed, or so we thought at the time.

I look around at the faces of the other Soldiers pulling "first-up" with me. Some are reading books, others are playing cards; all try to ignore the sweat sliding down their faces. My fellow Soldiers do whatever they can to take their minds off of the tremendous heat. Occupying down time is a craft at which every deployed Soldier becomes proficient. We have had only a few months practice and already we are experts.

Specialist David Campos: a large, tattooed, bear of a man who would rather be your best friend before your worst enemy, but you wouldn't know it by his size. Always the jokester, no matter how difficult the day, he is always there to brighten spirits.

Specialist Joe Brown: a deep thinker and one to always ask the most complex questions. Little did I know that later on in the deployment he would be one of two Purple Heart recipients from our platoon.

Private First Class Ricky Becktel: this is a guy who would do anything for you at the drop of a hat. Becktel is a strong Christian man who would love to tell you all about his little daughter waiting for him at home. He's exactly the type of person you want by your side in any combat medical situation.

Sergeant Ramon Santos: a short firecracker of an NCO. His rules are strict and his punishments even stricter. No one wants to disappoint him. He knows his job forwards and backwards which makes him a great teacher.

Suddenly, the yells of Staff Sergeant Black, my squad leader, pierce the hazy heat of the summer afternoon and find their way into my ears, startling me from my momentary peace.

"Get it up and get it on!" I shake the monotony from my head and quickly don my gear. I run to the vehicle and insure it is up and ready. I look in the patient transport area and do a quick mental checklist while I fight my way into my body armor and Kevlar.

"We have a 113 rollover outside the gate between here and Al Hitt. We don't know how many wounded or killed yet, I'm going to the TOC (Tactical Operational Command) to see if I can get more info. We are taking two tracks. Pete, you are driving me and SPC

Brown. Campos, you drive Becktel and SGT Santos. We need to be out of here in three minutes!"

We strap on the rest of our gear and make last minute checks to both tracks. Everything is as it should be. After a quick radio check I slide into the driver's hatch and fire up my beast. With a roar it responds. I look over at SPC Campos in the driver's hatch of the next track. As our eyes meet, we both know what this feeling is. It is the first hit of trauma related adrenaline for both of us. His look of confidence helps me overcome any apprehensions I may have felt. The sweat begins pouring profusely down my face and pools on my chest beneath my body armor. We anxiously wait for SSG Black so we can be on our way. The seconds pass like hours.

A few moments later SSG Black appears, jumps into my track and slides on his CVC (Combat Vehicle Communication) helmet. His voice crackles in my earpiece. "Let's go Pete, we don't have much time". With that, I slide my gear shift into 'drive' and press down hard on the accelerator. Again the metal beast responds and lurches forward. Once a call is placed, time is something we never have a lot of.

As our tracks roar out of the front gates of Al Asad and around the winding roads of Al Baghdadi, SSG Black updates me on the situation through our CVC's.

"A convoy heading for Al Asad had some 113's (tracked personnel carrier) in it." He yells into his CVC.

"Apparently one broke track and spun around, causing it to roll down an embankment. There is a bird en route to help us with evacuation. So far we know that the TC (Tank Commander) was thrown from the vehicle and he is in pretty bad shape. There are still Soldiers trapped inside, that's what I want you to focus on."

Various words echoed in my head. *"Pretty bad shape"*, *"trapped"*, *"you"*. My orders were clear and it is time to execute.

As we make our way to the rollover site I begin doing the two things that I feel comfortable doing. Rehearsing my training and praying. For the first time, I am outside the wire treating patients. This is it. It is now time to put to the test everything that I have learned. I wonder if I am up to the task. *"God, help me do my best"*.

Paintings of Saddam Hussein and the glares from the townspeople of Al Baghdadi didn't give me that "warm and fuzzy" feeling inside that I really needed. With a possible ambush at every turn and the fear of an IED exploding in my face at any moment, I try to stay focused. Even the children make me nervous. They run right up to my 13 ton vehicle as if they are tempting fate. I try to stay focused on the mission at hand. I am green, I know that. But that doesn't mean I have to act green.

We finally approach the rollover site and the scene is chaotic at best. A UH-60 Blackhawk medical evacuation helicopter has set down, stirring up sand that stings our faces. Medical supplies are scattered about as if an aid bag had exploded. Officers are screaming directions and the grunts pull perimeter security, occasionally glancing back over their shoulders to watch the madness. Besides the flight medic from the bird, there appear to be no medics present whatsoever. I slam on the brakes of my track and lower the rear ramp. It hits the ground with a thud, spreading more dust and sand in the air. It is time to go to work.

Trial by Fire

SSG Black hits the ground first and begins to take control of a very messy situation. I grab my aid bag and sprint down the 10 foot embankment; all the while I begin to survey the scene. I try to listen for screams, but the helicopter's thundering rotors prevent any human cries from reaching my ears. I make my way to the overturned vehicle.

As I run, I glance out of the corner of my eye. On the ground is the TC who has been thrown from the track. Soldiers are busy performing CPR, but it is to no avail. SSG Black tends to him the best he can, so I move on. SGT Santos and I climb inside the overturned 113 tracked vehicle. Now I hear the screaming. Smashed between two shelves that are only large enough for a man half his size is a Soldier. His legs are twisted around the TC seat and his raspy voice cries out for his mother and his men. The best way to demonstrate his plight would be to place an egg in a metal box and send it crashing down a hill. The result of that experiment creates a better analogy than I can describe.

After establishing that airway and breathing are sufficient (due to his constant screaming), we begin to devise a plan to extract him from the vehicle without causing any further back or neck injury to our patient.

I calmly speak to our patient. "My name's Joshua. SGT Santos and I are gonna get you out of here as soon as we can! We are going to work as fast as we can, but we need your help." I search for any trace of acknowledgement on his face to know he understands me, but I am unsuccessful in finding it.

"Where are my Soldiers?" He cried. "Oh my God it's my fault... I...my legs..."

He starts to go unconscious. The sweat stops falling from his brow and he begins to look too pale for my liking. We have enough problems without worrying about shock.

Just then SSG Black appeared in the doorway of the ramp. "What do you need?"

Somehow, between SGT Santos and me, we placed an order of oxygen, short spine board for extraction, and a traction splint for his right leg. As we wait for our needed equipment I begin asking those standing around for someone to get me a close friend of his. We need this Soldier conscious so he can give us the needed details about his pain so we can treat him accordingly. Within minutes our equipment is tossed to us.

As SGT Santos begins strapping on the short spine board used for extrication. I begin to cut off the Soldier's clothing so we can get a good idea of what is going on with our patient. As my trauma shears slice through his boots, I begin asking him what he can feel. In the background, I can hear one of his battle buddies talking to him and encouraging him.

"I can't feel anything down there!" He said as he began to squirm.

I feel his bare foot. Ice cold. I check his toe nails for capillary refill. *Nothing.* This is a problem. The first thing I suspect is a broken femur. The fractured bone had either severed or put significant pressure on the femoral artery, reducing blood flow to his lower leg. Now we are working against time. The femoral artery supplies the leg with a large amount of blood and is about as thick as a little finger. Not a situation that can be dealt with fully in the field.

Just then, SSG Black appears at the rear door of the destroyed vehicle we are inside of. He had taken control of the situation outside and is asking if we need any more equipment.

"I need a traction splint, and another bottle of oxygen!" I yell before I even had time to process his question. With a quick glance downward, I noticed Black had already provided us with the needed supplies. The thumping of the nearby evacuation helicopter echoes loudly within the twisted metal confines of the track.

"The bird is here, we have to get this guy out of here now!" He yelled at me over the roar. With a nod, I turn back to our patient and see that the extrication spine board has been put in place and he is ready to be moved from the vehicle. I begin talking to him again.

"We are gonna move you out. We'll do our best not to cause you any further pain but just bear with us, okay?" I didn't get the response I was looking for. The intense heat and severe pain of his injuries had caused our patient to become very groggy and nearly unconscious.

"Hey! Get that oxygen set up and in here now!" SGT Santos screams. The long spine board is set down inside the vehicle and we move the large Soldier onto it. The heat is getting to me. As I strap the patient down and secure his gear, the sweat is racing down my face and falling on his uniform. Dehydration is setting in and I begin to get dizzy. The screams of Soldiers and the pounding of the helicopter's rotors begin to sound distant and garbled. I feel myself slipping away. If I could just close my eyes...

"THWACK!"

The hard, swift slap of SGT Santos' hand across my helmet wakes me from my trance. He saw that I was about to pass out and helped me in classic SGT Santos style.

"Not right now, you skinny bastard!" He says with a smile. "We'll have time to go to sleep later, now help me carry this guy out of here."

"Thanks." I said, squinting the sweat out of my eyes, "I'm good, let's move him out."

As SSG Black, SGT Selvera, SPC Campos and I move the patient out of the track I am hit in the face with sand being kicked up from the helicopter. It sticks like paste to my sweat-drenched form. With speed and determination, we apply the traction splint for his leg and initiate an IV to replace the lost fluids. We carry him to the bird and follow the crew chief's instructions on where to place him. As the bird is preparing to take off, I take one last glance at my patient. He is quiet now, except for the tears steadily streaming down his face. This thirty-something year old man is now a lost and hurt little boy. I yell a prayer into his ear and clasp his hand in mine. He affords me a smile and closes his eyes for the short ride to the hospital at Al Asad.

We attend to the two other wounded Soldiers. Amazingly, the driver is unhurt and the other passenger only sustains a sprained ankle. After treating his ankle on the scene, we load up and make our way back to Al Asad.

***

Upon arriving at the hospital, we hear the angry screams of someone inside. A Kevlar helmet flies from the inside of the hospital with two visibly shaken Soldiers following close behind. The helmet lands at my feet and quickly spins to a stop.

"Damn it! Why!?" The sobs of a Lieutenant reach my ears. He has just lost one of his squad leaders – the TC of the vehicle that I had just been inside of. The memories of that Soldier lying on the sand as medics worked on him resurfaced in my mind.

I watch as another Soldier tries in vain to comfort the fallen Soldier's platoon leader. He paces around crying and pleading, until finally sitting on the sandy concrete of the hospital's back steps. As I watch the officer cry on the shoulder of his fellow Soldier, I realize how serious my situation is. Because of a simple malfunction of a vehicle, a man is dead. There was nothing we could have done to save him. This was one of the many difficult realities that I would learn to accept as a medic in the war zone.

As I look back at this incident, I think about how much it affected me. The emotions that I felt that day are indescribable. I was afraid, confident, nervous and strong. The leadership of my NCO's and camaraderie of my fellow Soldiers fashioned within me a new and essential desire to give aid on the battlefield. I learned to keep my cool and take control in urgent situations. An example perfectly laid out for me by SSG Black at the scene.

While this incident was not due to combat injuries, it is still a situation in which today's Combat Medic finds himself. I would have many more opportunities to practice my craft throughout my tour in Iraq in the months to come, but none would have been as successful if I hadn't taken the feeling of fear that I had that day and turned it into resolve for staying true to those on *my watch*.

CHAPTER FOUR

Body Bag Detail

War is an ugly thing, but not the ugliest of things. The decayed and degraded state of moral and patriotic feeling which thinks that nothing is worth war is much worse. The person who has nothing for which he is willing to fight, nothing which is more important than his own personal safety, is a miserable creature, and has no chance of being free unless made or kept so by the exertions of better men than himself.

--John Stuart Mill

11 September 2003

It's 0200. Wait, maybe it's 0300. I'm still not sure what time I was awakened from my much needed sleep. I thought I would get used to the odd hours pulled by a medic, but every middle-of-the-night call comes as a surprise. I should know better, war doesn't sleep. This is especially true in the town of Ar Ramadi. My Regiment has been in the location running missions for the last four months. Recently, the 82nd Airborne Division has been involved as well. To date many high value targets have been detained by Coalition forces in this volatile area of the "Sunni Triangle". Whatever enemy hasn't been captured yet makes his presence known through nocturnal attacks. The call to prayer over the town's loud speakers coupled with small arms fire is the typical lullaby.

It seems I had just drifted to sleep. I had finally found the one spot in my cot where it didn't squeak when I moved, and the conversations of the medics on duty had died down. I needed plenty of sleep because my assignment for tomorrow morning is driving our ambulance back to Al Asad to transport three routine patients. I have driven the route many times, but the towns of Al Hit-Haditha and Al Baghdadi are never the friendliest of places for a convoy. Tomorrow, we would pass through both.

Sleep. At long last. Now I could relax and put one more day under my belt. Another day closer to being home with my family and loved ones. I should have known it was too good to be true. Subconsciously, I heard the sound of pounding feet shortly before my eyes were invaded with a flashlight to my face.

A random voice shouts, "Everybody up! An infantry raid in town went south and we've got some of our boys coming in! Get up! We don't know how many and we don't know how bad!"

I blindly search for my glasses and stumble out of my cot. I clumsily circle my area looking for all of my necessary gear. As soon as I gather my scattered thoughts I help rouse the rest of the medics as we head for the aid station. A young Private runs past me as I am trying to run and tie my boots at the same time.

"Mass Cal (Mass Casualty Situation) Pete!" He says, as he struggles to put on his latex gloves. Those two words always mean serious business to us in the heart of the "Sunni Triangle".

"How many? What happened?" I ask, knowing full well that I should have asked for my own pair of gloves at the same time. The details would become clear to me soon enough.

"Our boys are stirring up shit in town..." the rest of his sentence trailed off as he made a sharp right into the aid station.

To my left I heard the radio squawking from the 577 tracked vehicle.

"At least three KIA's..." Not what I want to hear. I run into the aid station and grab a pair of gloves along with some airway adjuncts. Thunder Squadron medics are at the top of their game, but I figure it won't hurt to be prepared.

I work my way back to the radio among the other medics so I can gather more information.

"Thunder MAS, Thunder MAS, we are inbound to your position with three wounded, three KIA's, break..." A brief silence followed, even the sound of our own breathing is suspended.

"Bird is en route; our critically wounded are on their way to Al Asad, but we have three more for you that are pretty banged up. At your position in five minutes, out."

The demanding tone on the other end suggested the seriousness of the Soldiers we had coming in. Just as foretold, five minutes later our job began.

With a cloud of dust surrounding them, they peel around the corner past the TOC (Tactical Operations Center) to our aid station. Our casualties have been placed unconventionally in the back of HMMWVs, a side effect of fighting an unconventional war. I grab the closest Soldier next to me, along with a couple litters and run to their trucks. On the way, I train my ear to listen to the medical details and refine the needed information.

"Two gun shot wounds, left upper leg! He's got severe bleeding!" Someone yells amongst the clanking of rifles and the shuffling of gear.

"Shrapnel in the neck, get a nose trumpet over here! Gun shot wound, right shoulder. We have it dressed and the bleeding has slowed down but keep an eye on it!"

My eyes dart around the back of the truck while making my own assessments. The wounds are already exposed and dressings are applied when there is time. We lift the first patient onto the litter with the fragility of a newborn. Morphine and adrenaline have him so high he doesn't feel much pain yet. As he is loaded onto the litter, a flashlight sweeps the bed for any gear that was left behind. The bed of the truck is filled with blood. The blood sloshed and splashed with every bounce of the road, painting the entire bed an eerie crimson color.

After the patients are strapped to the litters and all interventions are checked, we move them inside the aid station. Everyone has a task. Medics, doctors and battle buddies dance around each other like a scripted ballet. As our doctor rechecks the interventions made by the medics on the scene, I initiate an IV. Pain and fear coat the faces of the wounded Soldiers lying in our care. Voices overlap one another in the aid station, yet all commands are heard and executed by the intended medics.

"What are my vitals for this one?"

"Keep pressure on this wound!"

"I want this IV opened up all the way! Prep the morphine!"

I step back and survey the scene, looking for anything not yet done. The same abruptness that started this evening appears to be ending it. Everything is quickly under control. These three are going to make it home.

I make my way outside and fill my lungs with the heavy Iraqi air. I begin to get a headache as the adrenaline wears off. SSG Lincoln, the Thunder Aid Station NCOIC (Non-Commissioned Officer In Charge) stands next to me, taking an extremely long drag on his cigarette. I yawn and ask him if he wants me to do anything else before turning back in. "We need a medic to tend to the KIA's," he says as the exhaled smoke traces his words.

"Are they ours or theirs?" I ask, almost as if the pleading in my voice would make the dead ones "theirs." Then I realize I started to sound scared, so I straightened my posture and listened for his answer.

"I don't know. You know what to do, bag them for transportation out of here."

"Roger that." I say, feeling the adrenaline starting to kick in again. I stop by the back of one of our HMMWVs and grab three body bags. The bags have a familiar smell. Like plastic, but with something else, ghastly and unnamable.

"It's just in your head." I say out loud to myself as I walk to the back of the aid station. I turn the last corner behind the building and I see a couple of non-medical Soldiers there to help me. I look down at the twisted pile of flesh in front of them. They look so out of place behind our aid station.

"That's only three?" I ask, almost certain there were too many body parts to belong to only three men. The pile gave me a disgusting feeling of relief. We don't pile our dead that way, these were enemy kills.

"Okay, let's straighten out this pile and see who needs Motrin", I say, sheepishly laughing, so I won't gag on the familiar smell of death. Luckily, the Soldiers laugh more than I do, so I feel a little more at ease.

The moonlight casts an eerie glow into the open eyes of the top man. It is as if every nightmare of death has become reality in a moment. Reluctantly at first, I grab his arms and instruct one of the nearby Soldiers to grab his feet. His flesh feels cold in my hands, but somehow I still feel as though this man, lying in the pitiful pose of death, could still wake at any moment and attack me, getting his revenge.

"Ready? One, two, three." We lift in unison. It would have been a successful move had the man's flesh, muscle and hand not popped off into my hand, splattering my raised arm hairs with blood. The fluid splash felt warm and heavy on my skin. He falls to the ground causing a hollow thump sound that caused my mouth to salivate. I choke down the vomit. I toss his arm on the ground and we half slide, half drag the man on top of the first bag and zip it up.

"Place him in the truck." I say, watching two of the Soldiers lift the lifeless form into a HMMWV. The Soldiers turn their faces up and away as if the extra few inches will save their noses from the rotting smell.

Suddenly, I hear the sound of violent emetics. The vomit added nicely to the concoction that lay at my feet. I look down and see that I forgot to load the hand that slipped off along with the patient.

"It's just a hand." I blurt out as if none of this bothers me and a dead man's hand gives me a repulsive handshake everyday. With every comment that I make I realize how pitiful my attempts are to cover up how disgusting this event really is.

"No," he wheezes, "that". - And points to the pile.

Immediately the smell got even worse. It takes my eyes a second to adjust and decipher exactly what I'm seeing. A gun shot wound to his abdomen had caused an evisceration. Nothing too terrible, just a little exposed intestine. My eyes follow the neck upward and the urge to vomit becomes even worse. The man didn't have much of a head. He possessed his right eye, half his nose and complete mandibular jaw. I curiously look into the empty cavity that once held thoughts of killing guys like me. The mandibular jaw made an interesting bowl shape. In that bowl existed plenty of blood, a little gray brain matter, and one eye ball floating in the middle of the mess like the last letter in alphabet soup.

"How is this guy's eye still hanging around when he lacks the whole part of his head that supported it?" I don't know if I said that out loud or just thought it. Judging by the "I don't know how you medics do this" look on the other Soldier's faces, it must have been out loud.

"Okay, let's get this guy bagged and try not to lose that eye right there." I wonder how my words did not bother me.

"How does this not bother you?" The other Soldier asks, almost reading my mind. I ignore the comment, simply upset that he read my mind. I'm a medic, this kind of thing isn't supposed to get to me. We place the man in the bag and load him just as the one before.

I turn around for the last man and the squeamish Soldier almost vomits again. The last one is lying there, washed in moonlight, arms cocked and legs placed as if he was jumping. *Didn't jump high enough I guess.* I try to think about anything else besides what I am doing before the whole nightmare gets to me. His entire digestive system is lying on the ground next to him.

"Mortuary Affairs will want all of this, so load it all in the bag." I didn't honestly think they cared to see it either but it had to go somewhere. I pick up his entrails with two gloved hands and place them in the body bag. His guts twist and turn in my hands as if trying to make their final escape. After the bodies are loaded, I decide by now they no longer need me at this scene, so I return to the aid station.

"We lost two." The NCOIC tells me as I begin washing and sanitizing my arms from the elbows down. I sigh deeply, as if that would lift the heaviness of my thoughts from my chest.

It is difficult to get all the blood off my skin. It's almost as if it is trying to burrow back into a living body. I hate the fact that

American blood and the blood of our enemy has mixed and danced together on my arm hairs. I sit down after a good fifteen minutes of scrubbing. I scrubbed my arms until my arms were redder than the blood that had previously found a home there. I am not sure how I am supposed to feel. We may have taken three bad guys, but it cost us American lives as well.

Neither crying nor laughing seems appropriate. I feel both of these emotions, but it is too difficult to do both or to give in to either. I wonder if it would be easier just to vomit. I dismiss all strategies of coping choices for the time being, and I just sit down and ponder my evening as the sun begins to chase the moon from the night sky.

It is during times like these when I really wonder what my family is doing at that moment. I have spent my night digging through corpses. They have no idea what I have just done. I wonder if I will ever tell them. I wonder if anyone will ever understand. I would have plenty of time to debate these questions in my mind while we convoyed back to Al Asad in as little as two hours.

CHAPTER FIVE

Pinned Down

Let every nation know, whether it wishes us well or ill, that we shall pay any price, bear any burden, meet any hardship, support any friend, oppose any foe to assure the survival and the success of liberty.

--John F. Kennedy

22 September 2003

Malaria infested mosquitoes, barking dogs and the nightly mortar attack is how I remember my time at Ar Ramadi. All three of these annoyances actually made my time there somewhat predictable, although not comfortable. Our position is an old Iraqi military post. Old uniforms and military metals once littered the floors of the building the Third Squadron, 3rd Armored Cavalry Regiment converted into an aid station. The Euphrates River splits the town in two, giving the area more vegetation and more mosquitoes, very unlike the rest of the barren country. It's September and the notorious heat is giving no signs of letting up anytime soon. The sand fleas make a living playground out of my epidermis at night as the sweat pools in my ears. Nevertheless we find ways to make our time there more comfortable. Thoughts of home are always in the back of our minds while we search for ways to ignore it.

While at this base, our job is to provide medical assistance and evacuation to all missions in and around the town of Ar Ramadi. If we have guys engaged in the city who need medical assistance, my NCO and myself grab our gear, meet up with security at the front gate, and run to get them as fast as we can in our four-litter ambulance HMMWV.

On the night of the 22nd I find myself outside of the aid station participating in the nightly game of Spades. Conversation around the table is typical: The cars we are going to buy when we get back to the real world, the first beer we are going to drink and with whom we are going to have it. The radio squawks occasionally as the gate guards check in with their report. It is a typical night. In fact, the only thing unusual about tonight is that it is approaching 2100 and all is quiet. It seemed almost too quiet for a night in the "Sunni Triangle." The only noise besides the boisterous conversation we all are sharing is the call to prayer over the loud speakers in town.

It was all too good to be true. The relative quiet of the evening was shattered as our radio blared. "THUNDER MAS, THUNDER MAS! (Third Squadron's Main Aid Station) This is Thunder X-Ray, we have just received word that our TCP (Traffic Control Point) team has just come under attack, break." We all freeze; it is time to go to work.

"Hostiles have employed at least one IED (Improvised Explosion Device) and followed the attack with small arms fire. There are two, possibly three casualties. Send your ambulance crew to the front gate to link up with QRF (Quick Reaction Force). You will proceed from there to the attack site."

My NCO and I exchange glances. We have a system that gets put into motion the second we receive a call. We both run and get our gear. Flack vest, body armor, Kevlar helmet, 210 rounds, and aid bags. All of my gear adds weight to my already humidity-soaked desert camouflage. While he runs and gets the details of our mission, I do last minute checks to the vehicle. All medical equipment and mechanical equipment must be ready to go at any given time so this step usually goes off without a hitch. Off we go.

The Physician's Assistant and a medic from the aid station jump in the back of our ambulance as we tear off towards the front gate. My NCO makes radio contact with QRF, alerting them that we are on our way to meet them. As I take the windy dusty roads a little faster than I should, I go over my medical algorithms in my head. I consider the injuries that we might encounter: Blast burns, GSWs (Gun Shot Wounds), amputations and so on. I go through my medical ABC's in my head as I pray for the strength to get me through what has the potential to be a very bad situation. I could not have been more right.

We skid to a stop at the front gate. QRF consists of about eight or nine HMMWVs loaded with Soldiers, weapons facing out. All of the Soldiers have the same look on their faces. Cold, determined, and ready for action. The PA springs from the back of my ambulance and gets in the back of the HMMWV directly in front of us.

"Listen up!" An important looking Captain shouts.

"It's still hot out there! We have at least one KIA; bird is en route to pick him up if we can get them to stop shooting at us for one damn second. We still have our TCP team pinned down, so be prepared to go in hot if we need to. Watch your buddy out there, let's go!"

"It's still hot out there!" The words enter my ears and sink to my stomach. I move my M-16 assault rifle to the window facing out.

"You scared Pete?" My NCO asks me with a little tremble in his voice.

"A little", I said fully knowing I just made the largest understatement of my life. I had not yet seen full fledged combat. It is time to put my training to work. I take a deep breath and painfully exhale. We get the "thumbs up" and we are off.

We tear through the streets of Ar Ramadi. At this point it's nearly 2200 and darkness rules the streets. The occasional street light illuminates glares on every street corner and my senses are on overload. Every twitch, every movement the locals make could be a potential life ending act. They all stare at me coldly. Not one of us wants the other to be around right now. It is an understood law that is made public only through looks of intimidation.

The heat is not unbearable, yet I'm sweating profusely. The sweat forms on my brow and takes a little journey around the edge of my Kevlar helmet before splashing down on my protective vest. Granted, it's around 100 degrees but I have gotten used to it. We cross the bridge that carries us over the Euphrates and take a winding left turn to the outskirts of town. We are taking turns so fast I think my vehicle may come up on two wheels. The road takes us back around to the river, away from what few town lights there are. There is no moon and stars are invisible. We shut off our headlights to avoid detection.

Up ahead on the road between the rows of tall grasses I see the Bradley fighting vehicle that has been hit. For the most part, the Bradley is still intact. If not for the blood on and around the vehicle, one may not even have surmised that it had been under attack.

"Good." I whisper to myself. "Maybe we can get our patients and get the hell out of here." Before I can even stop the vehicle I hear a Soldier scream, "CONTACT, CONTACT! Three o'clock!" Like rats from a sinking ship, Soldiers were jumping out of the backs of vehicles to find cover.

Before the next thought can enter my mind, I see tracer rounds zipping across my hood. "Thwap, dink, thwap!" Rounds are coming from everywhere to our right down by the river. My heart seems to stop as hot lead slices through the thick night air as quickly as a hot knife through butter. Time seems to stand still as my mind searches for the next action to take.

I have seen what a HMMWV looks like after a firefight and I knew I didn't want to stay in that vehicle. I throw on the parking brake and my tires whined in resistance as my ambulance comes to a fast halt. I throw open my door, grab my aid bag and M-16, and with one fluid motion, make a diving roll out my driver's side door. "Thwap, dink, thwap!" I make myself small behind my front left tire as the incoming lead seems to outline my silhouette. The sweat pours faster down my face. My lungs cringe with every rapid inhalation of the putrid air. This is it. My body and soul know that the next few responses that I make to the incoming rounds might end or save my life.

"Damn!" I scream to no one. I realize the medic we brought with us is still in the back of the ambulance with no stealthy way of retreat. If he attempts to exit out the back where the patients go in, he may as well just go ahead and zip himself up in a body bag first. I wriggle out of my aid bag and sling my rifle over my back. I jump back up through the driver's side door and unlatch the door in the middle of the vehicle so he can make his escape. It takes only seconds for him to join me in my tiny hiding place.

As he slides in next to me, I notice the same look of fear on his face that I am feeling in my gut. I help him out of his aid bag and point the best I can to where the fire is coming from. He rolls to the right side of the tire and assumes a prone firing position.

"Can we open fire?" He yells above the crackle of gunfire.

"Not yet!" I yell back. "We are still waiting on the 'go'."

"Anyone hit!?!" I yell over the incoming fire. *Silence.* That is good. I begin making a check of all my gear and looking for all the Soldiers I came with. By now my NCO and our other medic have made their way to my side of the vehicle. The PA has made his way to the Bradley. The smell of blood and death hung heavy in the oppressive air. It is a smell that I am becoming all too familiar with and the odor seems to intensify with the humidity.

I attach my NVG's (Night Vision Goggles) to my helmet and risk a glance around the side of the tire. The greenish tint of my goggles makes the scene appear as if it were mid-day and the bad guys are hurling flames in our direction. I detect no movement except for the flash of their muzzles. They are everywhere and nowhere.

I put my goggles away for fear of killing my body's own night vision altogether. "They knew more of us would be coming! We're sitting ducks up here on this ridge; do we have the 'go' to return fire?" I scream to anyone that would answer.

"Negative! Do not return fire! We have an LRS (Long Range Surveillance) team out there somewhere!" A Lieutenant screams above the noise.

"Damn it! We can't just sit here!" I yell in desperation. This whole idea of not firing back didn't make much sense to me. If we have a team in the vicinity, I would really appreciate it if they would lay down fire on our behalf.

My heart sinks as I realize we are pinned down. We can't risk shooting in the same direction some of our own may be positioned in. I make myself comfortable with my command's decision and accept our fate. It is going to be a long night.

"I'm going to see if there are any more casualties from the IED." I told my NCO. And with that I stay low and make my way down the row of vehicles until I arrive at the explosion site.

The small arms fire is dying down a little, with only a few sporadic shots here and there making their way to our position. Our PA has already found a way for the bird to land and evac the KIA.

"Any more casualties, sir?" As soon as I ask I see two Soldiers sitting next to him covered in blood. The pale looks on their faces clearly tell they had an experience with death tonight.

"Take these two back to the ambulance with you, they aren't wounded but they were in the Brad that was hit. Get an IV started with both of them and clean them up if you can. Get their vitals and information. I'll check them out when we get back to the aid station. I'll be back there in a few."

"Roger that, sir." And with that I motion to the two men and they eagerly follow me. On my way back to my HMMWV I think about how terrible it must be for these two. They are covered in the blood and brain matter of their battle buddy. There is no way that I can fathom their loss. I guide them back to my ambulance, keeping a wary eye on the occasional muzzle flash coming from the valley below.

After we are seated beside my ambulance, my NCO initiates IV's while I get their baseline vitals and information. The younger of the two Soldiers begins to cry as the effects of what has just happened begin to set in. The older just seems dazed, with a long stare of disbelief in his eyes. I continue with my medical screening. I find myself having to shout so they can hear me. Hearing loss is not uncommon in IED attacks.

Out of nowhere a loud 'WHOOSH' trumps the sound of incoming gunfire. All of us dive flat against the earth. The entire sky lights up like day. An illumination flare, fired by our Soldiers to expose the enemy's position. As the bright light invades the night sky, eerie shadows dance around the palm trees. I gather myself and brush the dirt off my face. I notice both of the Soldiers in my care are still lying on the ground. The sound of the flare has shaken them pretty badly; the effect of combat stress has taken its toll on them. I kneel down by them and help them sit up against my vehicle. I say a silent prayer in my heart. I ask for guidance from

God Above so that I may be the best encouragement and help to these psychologically wounded Soldiers.

These two Soldiers and I pass the next three hours chatting and exchanging stories about home. I try my best to take their minds off of the circumstances. This proves to be quite difficult since about every ten minute interval another burst of gunfire causes us to take cover. We are still waiting on permission to return fire. Permission never comes.

Two squads are sent out to recon the area after the gunfire has died down. At the enemy position blood is found where the Bradley had initially returned fire after being hit, but unfortunately, no enemy bodies. During the attack, hostiles had even maneuvered their boats up the Euphrates to get a few pot shots off at our position. Tonight it seems the popular thing to do as a resident of Ar Ramadi is to grab a weapon and head down to the river to get a few shots off at the Americans. Not exactly my idea of recreation.

The recon squads raid a few houses in the area and detain a few suspects, but nothing solid. Around 0130 we load up our vehicles with our patients and make our way back to our compound. Everyone is on edge for the drive back. We stop five times to investigate suspected IED's that may have been set up for our return. All turn out to be harmless pieces of trash. After a night such as this, no one is going to take any more chances.

We never returned fire that night. Adding to the disappointment was that the LRS team turned out to be nowhere in the vicinity. The decision had to be made with determination in the good faith of avoiding fratricide. I am comfortable with that.

My first taste of combat turned out to be the longest night of my life. I had met the enemy in close combat and I had proven to myself that even in chaos, as long as you keep your head, order can exist and the mission can be executed. If asked, I would participate in that night a hundred more times. As long as I wear this uniform, it will be my duty, and it will be *my watch*.

CHAPTER SIX

The Darkest Day

The LORD is my shepherd; I shall not be in want. He makes me lie down in green pastures, he leads me beside quiet waters, He restores my soul. He guides me in paths of righteousness for his name's sake. Even though I walk through the valley of the shadow of death, I will fear no evil, for You are with me. You prepare a table before me in the presence of my enemies. You anoint my head with oil; my cup overflows. Surely goodness and mercy will follow me all the days of my life, and I will dwell in the house of the LORD forever. **-- Psalm 23**

02 November 2003

On the morning of 02 November 2003, SPC Julius Gilfiley and I are finally leaving our unit for a much deserved three day R & R (Rest and Relaxation) trip. The idea of finally getting a break from missions and boredom is music to our ears. The plan is to board two CH-47 Chinook helicopters from Al Asad airbase and fly to Qatar by way of BIAP (Baghdad International Airport). I've never been a huge fan of flying but if I have to suffer for a few hours in the sky in exchange for three days of rest, I can deal with it. We had just received word two days before that we were going on the trip and we could think of nothing else. Needless to say, we are quite excited about our chance to have time to let off some steam in a safer environment after nearly eight months in the pressure cooker of the combat zone.

Gil and I have grown closer over the past few weeks. While at Al Asad, the medics in my platoon are in charge of teaching CLS(Combat Lifesaver) classes. These classes are designed to teach non-medical personnel basic battlefield first aid so that they may keep their comrades alive and stable until medical help can arrive if none is immediately available. These classes also teach Soldiers how to work with and assist the medics that are already on the scene of a trauma. Gil had just graduated from our week long course two days before the trip. Little did I know that the knowledge that he gained from those classes would save lives in just as little as two days after his graduation. Gil is a NBC (Nuclear Biological Chemical) specialist assigned to our troop. Any medical knowledge that he possessed was received just the week before. I thank God every day that he paid attention in class.

Gil and I wake up around 0500 with all of the needed gear to make our three day trip. Not much is needed; shower items and one pair of civilian clothes. With my eyes still groggy from the little sleep I had the night before, my NCO and I load up all our gear and we drive to the flight line where the Chinooks sit ready to begin the hour long flight to BIAP (Baghdad International Airport). As we sign on for the trip, and sit around with the others bound for leave to the states for R & R, we talk about how nice it is going to be to leave behind all the stress associated with military medicine for three days. I look around at the other Soldiers waiting with us. For so early in the morning, their spirits are up and all of us are ready to go.

The SOP (Standard Operating Procedure) for these R&R trips is to leave our weapons with our unit at Al Asad. Not only are weapons required to be left, but aid bags and body armor is also encouraged to be left behind. I made the decision to leave both along with my weapon. I notice Gil brought his body armor and a little pouch with a standard field dressing. My NCO and I kid him a little. "You can leave that here man, we're not running missions." Words I never thought I would regret saying. "I think I'll hang onto mine" he said, "you never know." Truer words have never been spoken.

***

As our flight time of 0730 approaches we are escorted out to the flight line. I have never really enjoyed flying. I have buddies who are helicopter mechanics and I had heard too many horror stories to feel at ease. I always thought if the good Lord intended me to soar through the air I would have been issued wings at birth. Nevertheless, these birds are going to get us out of Iraq for a while, so I try not to let it bother me too much. As we receive the flight brief from the pilots and the crew chief, Gil and I decide that we want to sit towards the rear of the lead bird. We try to count out how many people needed to go in front of us so we would be placed by the rear ramp that is lowered during flight to accommodate the rear gunner. While Gil is counting heads, I notice that the bag I have chosen to carry my gear in looks exactly like everyone else's.

This wouldn't be so much of a problem if we all held onto our bags, but the procedure for flights is to palletize luggage.

"I wish I would have brought some tape to tie off on my bag." I whisper. "We'll be spending our first few hours of R & R sorting out bags." Right then Gil jogs off about 40 meters to hunt down a little piece of orange plastic that is fluttering across the flight line.

The fact that there even is trash on the flight line is absolutely unheard of. Trash is always policed up regularly to protect the engines of the aircraft. If a piece of wayward trash were to fly up into the engine, a bird could be rendered useless.

At the time I said, "Hey, thanks man." If I would have known how that little orange piece of plastic would permanently change my life I would have said a lot more than that. My father would later tell news cameras that this little piece of orange trash was "part of an angel's wing."

The bit of time that it took me to tie that little piece of brightly colored plastic trash to my bag for easy identification cost us our place on the lead aircraft. They took two other Soldiers and filled the seats we wanted. Those of us who didn't get on the first aircraft were ushered to the second one. "Oh well," I said to Gil, "they are both going to the same place." As it turns out, Gil is placed by the rear ramp and I am seated next to him. All is going well. What we couldn't know is how very different the same flights were to be for these twin Chinooks.

The scheduled flight pattern for the two CH-47's was one that has been traveled countless times before. The flight plan had us departing Al Asad at 0730 and arriving at the 82nd Airborne controlled

M.E.K. compound on the outskirts of Al Fallujah about twenty-five minutes later. This stop was scheduled so we could pick up two more passengers along with some communications equipment. We are briefed beforehand that the Chinooks can make it as far as Baghdad before they have to refuel, but there isn't a lot of time to spare so the stop has to be quick. From the M.E.K. we are to proceed to BIAP. This route takes us over the towns of Ar Ramadi and Al Fallujah, two very dangerous spots for coalition troops. From BIAP we would then travel to CENTCOM (Central Command) Headquarters in the country of Qatar for our three days of R & R.

Just as planned, around 0730 we have "wheels up" and we are on our way. During our briefing, the pilots inform us of the short stop at the 82nd Airborne M.E.K. compound near Al Fallujah. Right on schedule, we departed the M.E.K. compound around 0830.

My attention is completely riveted out the back ramp as we ascend to our altitude of approximately 300 feet. We are right over the Euphrates now. It looks so lush and green, almost emerald in color. There are palm trees lining the banks and small fishing boats perusing the river. I am thinking to myself how beautiful it looks. Most of Iraq is barren desert and before long, one grows to hate everything that has to do with sand. But as we soar over the river, I am reminded of the Bible stories that were told to me as a boy. This part of Iraq fits all the images of such stories that I had conjured up in the mind of my childhood. I try to tell Gil how pretty I think it looks but the incredibly loud thumping of the Chinook's twin rotors keep me from conveying much of anything besides arm signals. The scenery has momentarily taken my mind off how much I dislike flying. My stomach finally settles and I am more than ready for a few days of relaxation and free phone calls home to the States. I settle back in my seat and watched the rear gunner proceed with his mid-flight checks. I feel my eyes growing tired from the early morning wake-up and I decide to try to get some sleep. The thought of speaking to my parents and girlfriend again soon brings peace to my soul. This would be the last bit of peace that I would feel for a long time.

***

Gil begins pounding on my arm. I look at him, almost angry at him for destroying my two seconds of solitude. As my eyes meet his, I instantly read the look of sheer terror on his face. His normally brown skin is ghostly white. He is pointing towards the town of Al Fallujah below. As I look, I see what appears to be a trash fire on the ground with a vertical trail of black smoke. I wonder if he thinks it is an RPG (Rocket Propelled Grenade). Eight months in Iraq has taught me that the vapor trail from an RPG is whitish in color. This smoke is black, so we have nothing to worry about, until suddenly the smoke changes direction and begins heading directly toward us. I don't remember if I screamed or just closed my eyes. What I do remember is Gil laying his head in my chest. I instinctively put my hand around his shoulder as if to hug him good bye. In that instant we know we are going to die.

In those terrorizing seconds my mind drifts to home. I envision myself walking through the house I grew up in, sitting on my mother's lap and playing baseball with my dad. My whole life didn't flash before my eyes, as the saying goes, but memories of my childhood did. As I look up again I see the SAM (Surface to Air Missile) whiz by the right side of our aircraft. It is so close that as we bank to the right the smoke from the missile invades the passenger compartment of our aircraft.

"Holy shit!" is the inaudible scream that was unmistakable on the rear gunner's mouth as he witnessed what has just transpired. He scrambles to aim his weapon in the direction of the launch. The looks on all of the Soldiers' faces are the same: "This *can't* be happening!"

We all thought they were a poor shot and we lucked out. Unfortunately, they were better than we thought; the lead CH-47 was their target. Dread still grips my chest and I find breathing to be a chore. As our pilots see the engine of the lead aircraft explode, they guide our bird into a corkscrew evasive maneuver. We bank hard left and begin descending rapidly. As I look out the rear ramp from my seat, I see the tree tops and houses of Fallujah whiz by in a circular motion. This is it. I know they have reloaded and are now ready to shoot us down. My last few moments alive are going to be spent spinning and praying.

As we circle, the enemy opens up with small arms fire. Their AK-47 rounds pepper the inside of the passenger compartment, sending sparks down on our heads. Anti-missile flares begin deploying from our tail to distract anymore oncoming heat seeking missiles. Had I been able to hear over the thundering rotors, my ears would have been filled with shouts and screams of Soldiers on our bird. We all felt the presence of death inside our passenger compartment.

The crippled lead aircraft slams to the earth, bouncing twice before coming to its final resting place. The destroyed helicopter settles as burning debris and twisted metal in a farmer's field surrounded on all sides by irrigation streams and houses. The ground is muddy and due to palm trees and vegetation that is typical of the Euphrates area, visibility is limited, making enemy positions nearly impossible to detect.

Our pilots circle the crash site a few more times, searching for signs of life, hoping and praying that at least one Soldier has cheated death. We land hard at the crash sight - a very difficult and heart-wrenching decision for our pilot to make. We are unarmed except for one M-16 assault rifle and an automatic crew-served weapon on the rear ramp. R & R had officially ended: We are now in a combat situation. For all my pilots know, everyone on that downed bird is dead. Their decision to set our aircraft down in a "hot" situation without proper protection could have been a career-ending move. Our crew held fast to the ideal that, "**no Soldier is left behind**". They placed their lives and the lives of our entire crew in danger on the slim outside chance that we would be able to save whomever we could from the wreckage. I am thankful every day of my life that the pilots of my aircraft made that choice. Their decision to land saved many Soldiers' lives that day.

***

As soon as we hit the ground the rear gunner points to Gil and a Soldier sitting across from us to go check for survivors. The other Soldier grabs the only M-16 on board and heads out the back ramp, chambering a round as he ran. Gil follows closely behind.

One priority taught in the Army is that you watch out for your buddy. That includes parties on the weekends and on battlefields far away. When I see my buddy Gil leaving, I know there is no way I am going to let him go without me. My feet carry my body down the rear ramp before the command to do so even enters my brain. My mind had no regard for my personal well-being. My heart pounds with each step towards the wreckage. My life is in the hands of God as I proceed along with the two other Soldiers. Smoke fills my lungs. Sand stings my face. Adrenaline courses through my veins. It is a movie scene with no cuts.

As I run behind Gil to the crash site I see other people running off to our left. Small arms fire again. The rounds spray the sand between Gil and I as we run about 200 meters to what is left of the burning helicopter. For a fleeting second I experience fear on a level that I have never known.

"Sweet Jesus!" I pray. "You kept me alive this long for some reason, let me get to that bird so I can complete my job!"

The Soldier who exited our bird ahead of Gil and me begins laying down suppressive fire with the only 30-round magazine he has. Gil and I dive into the wreckage searching for the pilots who would have M9 handguns. Gil finally finds one and begins surveying our perimeter for any more hostiles. His screamed profanities are used as ammunition to ward off the advance of the encroaching hostiles. No real ammo can be found.

As I crouch in the wreckage, I begin looking around at the tangled mess of metal and flesh. Amputated limbs and bloody uniforms is all that my mind seems to grasp. I begin searching for any sign of life amongst the incredible amount of death. I try as hard as I can to turn off my heart's feelings and let my mind execute my mission. This proves to be much more difficult than I thought. It is then that the smell begins to saturate my being.

Any veteran who has spent time on the battlefield will tell you about the gruesome familiarity one obtains with the smell of death. It invades the nostrils and seems to live in the skin for days. It can't be showered off, it can't be wished off. It can't at all be ignored; it hangs heavy in the psyche for a very long time. It makes the heart sink, and no one who has ever smelled it could ever forget it.

Now I scream for anyone still alive to make some movement. At first, it is difficult to tell the difference between twisted metal and twisted bodies. In the background of my mind I listen to our only M-16 crack off rounds in the enemy's direction. I lay as low as I can in the rubble while I search for survivors. As my face roots through the pile I make a positive discovery. There is movement and cries for help! I can not believe how many people are still moving. There are approximately 32 passengers on the downed helicopter and I immediately see at least seven or eight Soldiers still alive.

"I need you to help me with the wounded." I scream at Gil, perhaps louder than necessary. Sweat pours down his face and his eyes dart about as he tries to calm himself and listen to what I am saying. His hands are shaking as badly as mine.

I grab his face. "I need you to focus and remember everything we just taught you last week. You have to help me! I cannot do this alone!" He swallows hard and immediately gains control. We both nod and we know what has to be done.

***

We start by dragging the first casualty we see away from the wreckage. Because the engine is still on fire and there are hostiles in the area, our priority is to get the living evacuated as soon as possible. It is very difficult for me to think of dragging these injured Soldiers around without taking the proper precautions I was taught just a short time ago at Fort Sam Houston. But this is war, not a textbook. We are under attack, the enemy is present, and our boys need to be moved away from that burning engine and an enemy who still desires to finish the job.

The screams and moans of the Soldiers around me harden my resolve to do whatever I can even without my medical equipment. I take a quick look around me to see how many are still alive and can be saved. Gil and I begin pulling as many Soldiers out of the area as we can. We create a system: I lift wreckage, Gil pulls the wounded out and drags them away from the burning wreckage as I give him quick lifesaving instructions. I tell him to keep yelling the status of every patient to me while I am working on the ones in the wreckage. With no medical gear available it is time to adapt and overcome. Gil and I begin tearing our T-shirts to use for bandages and dressings. We use parts of the downed bird for splints and tie them off with a cord from a CD player headset that we find in the wreckage.

I have Gil start on splinting for a few patients and I go back into the wreckage to see if I can get to a few more Soldiers. As I look to the bottom of the hot twisted mess, I notice a Soldier underneath many layers of bent steel. I reach to feel for a pulse.

My sweaty, now blood-soaked hands slipped about on his wrist. Finally, I found what I was looking for. He had a pulse, it was weak, but it was a pulse.

"Thank God!" I'm certain I said it out loud.

"Hey! If you can hear me move something! I know you are hurting but you have to give me a sign. We are working as fast as we can, just hold on!"

Nothing. I reach down to feel his chest. *Nothing.* I know I have to get my air into this Soldier if he is to stand a chance. I pull and pry at the metal blocking my way to his mouth. My mouth is inches from his face, inches between life and death. Tears well up in my eyes. I pull at the wreckage with all of the strength I can muster. It will not move.

I see what I believe to be a blood soaked duffle bag on top of the wreckage that is in the way of my reaching this man with air. As I try to reach my hand around the object to move it, I feel my hand get warmer and sink through the object. What I thought was a bag is in actuality the abdomen of one of my fallen brothers. As soon as I realize what I have done, I quickly pull my hand out and look at it. I want to cry. I want to go home. I want this all to go away. I want to hit the panic button and ask someone else to take over. I learned a few short months ago that as a medic you can't cry on the battlefield. You can't hit the panic button. As the only medic there, I *am* the panic button. With a sinking stomach and aching heart, I gently move the body aside and regain focus on the man I am trying to reach. Sadly, it wasn't to be.

With my lips inches from his mouth I had to complete the hardest task of the medic's job. I had to play God. I had to decide if spending more time on this unreachable Soldier who would have very little chance of survival would threaten another Soldier's life that I could save if I got to them now. I make my heart wrenching decision, I move on.

At this point I move to the outside of the wreckage to assess the ones that have been drug out so far. Soldiers are lying everywhere. Some are propped up on one elbow, holding bandages to their broken and torn bodies. A few are gasping for what would be their last few precious seconds of oxygen. I began to feel helpless.

"Where are those damn med evac birds!? I scream out loud in half prayer, half desperation. And where is our security?"

It seems we have been here for hours; the 82nd Airborne should have been here by now with medical support and security. It has only been 20 minutes. It is then I realize that it will be impossible for me to medically treat all of the casualties. A feeling of helplessness creeps into my soul. I begin utilizing the other passengers that were on my bird who have come to help. I instruct the females from our bird to sit with and talk to the ones who are in the most pain.

There is something about the presence of a woman that makes intolerable pain seem bearable. I believe our innate relationship with our mother affords this. I placed the females near the heads of the wounded. Some holding airways open, some I instruct on splinting and others are just there to be a comforting voice in the middle of incomprehensible chaos.

As various Soldiers speak comfort to the wounded and stabilize the cervical spine, I find whatever pieces of clothing and material I can to dress and bandage wounds. The largest complication we face is patients not having a patent airway. Facial trauma has caused bleeding on many patients and threatened to block the breathing of those struggling to hang on to what may be life's last few moments. Without suction equipment, the only alternative is to place Soldiers on their sides so that blood could be coughed out. This bought us time.

One of the next injured I see has suffered a broken lower arm and both of his ankles are broken so badly that the sides of his bloody boots are folded around and touching his lower leg. I grimace at the sight. The open fracture in his arm is piercing his cheek and creating a bleeding problem that threatens his breathing. Gil and I remove his destroyed bone from his cheek and lay him on his side so that he can cough the blood out. Without cutting tools, it is impossible to remove his boots without fear of his feet coming off with the boots. Gil constantly asks him to wiggle his toes and assure us that circulation is completing its course to his lower extremities after we splint his feet the best we can. There are more Soldiers still trapped, so I leave Gil to manage the wounded Soldier and I return to the destroyed aircraft.

We signal to our bird that we need more people to help us with all of the casualties, as we are finding still more living among the dead. Without regard for personal safety, all of the passengers download from our aircraft and begin helping in any way that they can.

Now all of the survivors that are still trapped have someone making an effort to pull them to safety. I yell instructions on how I want the patients triaged for the flight medics when they come to evacuate the wounded. All of the Soldiers pull together and give every wounded man and woman the best fighting chance that they would ever have. We are told that birds and Soldiers are inbound with med evac and security. I begin my search through the broken pieces for more survivors. I look down as I am crawling amongst the rubbish and I see two Soldiers that I had just spoken to before we left Al Asad. Both happy and full of life just an hour before, now paid the ultimate sacrifice in the middle of an Iraqi field. The contorted position of their twisted bodies haunts me to this day. I see them all in my dreams. This all has happened on *my watch*.

***

Like Angels from Heaven, the 82nd Airborne arrives. With a company sized element for security and med evac helicopters, there finally appears to be hope. They come to our rescue by helicopter and HMMWV. With them, they bring the much needed medical supplies. My prayers have been answered. The wounded are already triaged and ready for evacuation.

One young medic hops off one of the birds and comes running full force towards the scene. He takes one look at the images around him and vomits. I can't hesitate. Now, lying in the blood spotted sand in front of me are the medical supplies I have been praying for. I take his aid bag and dump the contents onto the ground. I begin handing out splints and bandages as fast as I can. I take all of the airway adjuncts that are available and begin inserting them into the patients who are literally dying for lack of them.

There are only so many litters, so the most critical are loaded on them and sent off to Baghdad in the Blackhawks as fast as we can move them. The Chinook that I arrived on is designated for the least critical. *Least Critical?* I doubt there is such a thing on a day like today.

With all the litters spoken for, Gil and I begin carrying patients to the Chinook. The first Soldier I lay hold of is a young sergeant. His lower leg is broken and he is very disoriented. I splint his leg the best I can and throw him over my shoulder, fireman-carry style. He screams in pain with every muddy, slushy step I take towards the Chinook. His screams vibrate through every inch of my body just like a jack hammer. My legs are burning from fatigue and I am high on adrenaline. With the strength that only this self defensive drug affords me, I carry him up the ramp and lay him down on the seats. I turn to go back to the crash site. He grabs my leg and begins to cry. His tears swirl down his face, collecting particles of sand and smudges of blood on the way down his cheek.

"It hurts so badly! My God, how the hell could this happen!?"

I turn around to him and fall to my knees on the floor of the bird by his face. If it weren't for my dark sunglasses, he would have seen the tears in my eyes as well. I shout to him over the thumping of the rotors.

"Listen, I need you to be strong right now." I said, with obvious tears in my voice. I'm not sure if I can finish my admonition. I swallow hard.

"There are a lot of people out there hurt worse than you; some won't even make it home. I need you to be strong for them. I need you to comfort every Soldier I place next to you in this bird. You may be the last voice they hear on this earth. 'Cowboy up' sergeant, we'll both have time to cry later if we want to."

With that, he straightens up and gives me a "Roger that." Both the intense pain that this Soldier feels in his body and the sorrow that tears at his heart for the other Soldiers is plastered on his face. Both of us know we will spend plenty of time crying later.

***

Unable to abandon our patients, Gil and I spend the next two hours carrying Soldiers to their evacuation aircraft. We carry, pull and yell until we cannot possibly continue. The 82nd has now taken full control of the situation. There are four OH-58 Kiowa helicopters circling our perimeter, a total of twelve med evac helicopters inbound and outbound and infantrymen protecting us on every side. Medical supplies and bloodied uniforms cover the ground.

"So this is what war is like." I say to myself. I do the best I can to repress the feelings of hatred that thrashed within me.

As my mind drifts through the horrid events of the past few hours, I am reminded of how close I have come to death. If it had not been for the God-given breeze that carried that little orange piece of plastic across the path of Gil and me, we would be on our way to Baghdad; either bloody and bruised or dead. I thank God everyday that He spared my life and placed me in a situation where I, with the assistance of every brave Soldier aboard my aircraft, could render the best aid that we could that morning.

Our dead are never forgotten. Respect for a fallen Soldier is our highest priority. It is the service and sacrifice of our lost brothers and sisters that gives us our blanket of freedom and prosperity. While the wounded are being flown out of the crash site, I stagger over to where we have laid those who made the ultimate sacrifice. The pieces of fabric covering their faces and bodies twitch and move with every incoming and outgoing helicopter. I kneel down beside the formation of fallen heroes. I find myself straightening their uniforms and wiping the blood from their faces. The glitter of one man's wedding band caught my eye and I just sit and stare. His wife doesn't even know yet. I reach down and wipe the dirt and blood off of his ring.

I feel lost in the moment, almost living outside of the experience. I know with everything within me that we had done everything possible to give each Soldier a second chance at life. That still didn't insulate me from the haunting that insisted on my asking myself time and time again over the next few months if I truly did everything I could. I didn't want to admit that not every one can be saved. I said a silent prayer for each one of those Soldier's families then and there. Weakness takes hold of my body as my staggering legs move me back to where they have started to report for accountability of our group.

I find standing to be too difficult so I crumple to my knees and then fall onto my back in exhaustion. Lying on the ground, I finally remove my Kevlar helmet, the only piece of protective equipment I was wearing during the catastrophe. As I roll over onto my side, I remove the items that I have carried with me in the top of my helmet for the last eight months. My blood-encrusted hands shake violently as I remove a dirty, wrinkled piece of paper that has Psalm 91 written on it. I immediately read it to myself again. Tears slowly run down the contours of my bloody, dirty face and make their way to the page in my quivering hands. I see a picture of my parents and brother whom, just hours before, I thought I would never see again. I study the mud soaked picture of Layla, my darling. She looks one hundred times more beautiful in that picture on this morning than she had ever before seemed to me. I kiss the picture for fear of never seeing her sweet face again. Finally, I read the lyrics to "Bridge Over Troubled Water," a little piece of home that she had mailed to me. A song that were just words to me at one time, mean so much to me now.

This letter was sent out to all of the 3d ACR Soldiers' family members back home from Colonel David A. Teeples, the 70th Colonel of the Regiment. He informs the families of the accomplishments of the Regiment, the vigilance of the Troopers and the estimation of our redeployment back to the States.

07 November 2003

Troopers and Families of the 3d Armored Cavalry Regiment:

The last seven months have been significant in the history of our Regiment. The Regiment has secured nearly a third of the country of Iraq. We are responsible for over 800 kilometers of international borders and four points of entry, two with Syria, one with Jordan, and one with Saudi Arabia. We have conducted operations across the spectrum of conflict, with Troopers fighting in close combat situations, as well as performing stability and support for Iraqi communities. Part of our mission is to prepare our area of operations for a Transfer of Authority (TOA) to other, follow-on Coalition Forces or Iraqi Security Forces.

A recent Department of Defense announcement outlines the force package for the second year in Iraq, termed Operation Iraqi Freedom II. The force package includes those units that will replace the Regiment in western Iraq and a sequencing of units for the TOA. The announcement indicates that our TOA may take place in March 2004 and following the TOA we will begin movement out of Iraq and to the port. Redeployment activities at the port will be intense as we ready our equipment for shipment back to Fort Carson. With the current timeline for our redeployment I expect the Regiment to return home in the month of April.

The news you hear and see still shows Iraq as a dangerous part of the world. The tragedy of 02 November deeply hurt the Regiment. However, we continue our mission here in Iraq remaining vigilant and prepared for any contingency. Our Family Readiness Groups continue to inspire us with their strength, faith, and unwavering support.

The holidays draw near and we face separation from our loved ones. My hope is that all will feel that the Regiment is their family. The 3d U.S. Cavalry is strong because of our devotion to one another.

Thank you all for the sacrifices you make everyday. Your service secures the gift of freedom for millions of people. God bless you all.

David A. Teeples
70th Colonel of the Regiment

CHAPTER SEVEN

The Cost of Taming a City

History has demonstrated that the most notable winners usually encountered heartbreaking obstacles before they triumphed. They won because they refused to become discouraged by their defeats.
--B. C. Forbes

20 November 2003

The recent Chinook incident caused a big stir within our Regiment. It was the largest loss of life we had suffered in a single day since the war began. Not only did our Regiment suffer loss, but because of the other units stationed with us, the tragedy touched the lives of many of our Squadron's support elements as well.

In the days and weeks that followed I numbly made my way through multiple memorial services for the fallen. With every stanza of 'Amazing Grace', on every bugle note of 'Taps' and at the end of every roll call for the dead, I cried like a baby. My sadness and depression were palpable.

It was after one of these services that Gil and I were approached by my Squadron Commander, Squadron Sergeant Major, and the Regimental Sergeant Major.

"We are so proud of you Soldiers." The Regimental Sergeant Major said in a voice comparable to James Earl Jones.

"You did the right thing. Many lives were saved on account of your actions."

I looked at Gil through my teary eyes. He looked back at me and his face reflected the very thoughts in my heart. I didn't feel proud. I don't even know if I did all of the right things. The fact was, I wasn't sure when I would even be ready to run another mission. I still jumped at the slightest sounds and my dreams were tormented with the smells of death. As my own thoughts began to hurl me further into the pit of despair in which I was already waist deep, my Squadron Commander addressed me:

"Specialist Peters, we have a large operation coming up around the Al Qa'im area. I would really like for you to accompany me as my personal medic. We will be stationary at FOB Tiger. That area has had a lot of enemy activity recently and I want you to come with me."

Well, there it was. I had already talked myself out of running any missions for at least a month and here I am with three of the four highest ranking Soldiers in my chain of command wanting me to go right back out. The thought of going outside of the wire again didn't set well on my already weak stomach. I wasn't sure how I would react under pressure again. What if I fold? What if I freeze and someone else pays the price?

"Yes ma'am, I'll be there." I couldn't believe those words just left my mouth. I'm surprised I didn't make a physical effort to reach out and grab the words before they reached her ears.

"Excellent. I'll tell your commander and you will get all of the details. We'll head out in a few days, get some rest."

And with that, the Sergeants Major and my Squadron Commander turned to leave as if wanting to escape before I could recant my decision. I looked back at Gil and neither of us said a word. We somberly walked back to our Troop's TOC.

True to her word, in a matter of two days I found myself in the back seat of my Squadron Commander's HMMWV on my way to Al Qa'im. As the vast desert whipped by my window I had time to contemplate the words of my squad leader during his brief to me concerning this mission.

This mission is dubbed 'Operation Rifles Blitz'. This endeavor involves the fighting elements from all four of our Regiment's fighting Squadrons. The object of the mission is to round up as many high value targets as possible and detain them for questioning and possible imprisonment. This means rounding up as many 18-60 year old males as we can find. The town of Al Qa'im is run like Chicago back in the mobster days. All of the town's officials are bought out and those with the largest guns are prosperous. The eclectic mix of criminals here is largely due to the town's proximity to the Syrian border. One of the favorite activities of the average Middle Eastern terrorist is to travel to this part of Iraq for his chance to take a few shots at Americans.

The innocent people are given a chance to leave. Flyers are dropped by air stating that townspeople have a certain window in which they are allowed to leave before the invasion begins. All of those who remain behind are subject to searches and confinement upon probable cause.

The mission is to be launched from FOB (Forward Operating Base) Tiger. This is an old train station occupied by First Squadron. Their Bradley fighting vehicles, M1 Abrams tanks, and various air powers are an impressive site. By working with the local law enforcement, they have kept a tight grip on insurgency in their area of operations around the city of Al Qa'im. Now it is time to bring the city itself under control.

After an uneventful three hour convoy to FOB Tiger, I download my gear and decide to head to the aid station to look up some medic buddies of mine who are there as medical support for the three day mission. With an operation as large as this one, we leave nothing to chance.

As I journey up the hill in the darkness, I pass defunct trains, many of which have graffiti sprayed on them broadcasting to the Soldiers what cars are off limits. Past the trains and tracks I find myself at the front of the train station, now the headquarters for this whole shindig. I see military ambulances so I know I'm in the right place. Before I have time to ask where my buddies are, I see SPC David Campos striding up to me.

"What the hell are you doing here?" He yells at me while snubbing his cigarette out on his boot.

"The SCO (Squadron Commander) asked me to come, I don't think I had a choice." I reply, just happy to be around my friend again.

After an unnecessarily long monologue about how I am now a "teacher's pet", SPC Campos pauses to light another cigarette. After a long exhale he says, "Well, it should be pretty busy the next few days so just stay around and help out."

The thought of volunteering for anything didn't sit well with me. I try to think of a way to casually side step his statement when I am interrupted by a HMMWV pulling up to the aid station and blood covered medics jumping out. *Here we go.*

The back of the vehicle drops open and its contents reveal medical supplies strewn about and the all too familiar smell of blood and sweat.

I peer inside and my eyes are met with an Iraqi man who is bleeding from his side. Breathing seems to be a chore for him and the look on his face combined with his indecipherable screams quickly explains the amount of pain he is suffering.

I feel less than nothing for this man. In my mind, it is he who put me through the worst day of my life just days before, he who had caused the deaths of so many Soldiers who were but one hour away from being able to escape this hellish environment for a few days. I had just committed one of the biggest sins in the war zone. I transferred my hate to this man. I grabbed the first medic that hopped out of the vehicle to find out what happened.

The pasty white complexion of the young Soldier told me he isn't use to seeing this sort of thing. By his lack of coherence and fidgety mannerism I guess it is maybe the first time he has seen blood in his life. I decide gathering information from him is futile so I just listen to the other medics give their report as the wounded man is carried into the aid station.

Apparently, he had set off an IED. Not just any IED. The special kind of IED that this man was rigging was complete with a bag of nails in front of the blast area so the shrapnel would rip through the flesh of any American in the vicinity. The convoy that brought him here opened fire and one of the rounds found its mark in the chest of this luckless person of questionable lineage. Thankfully, the blast from the road side bomb injured none of our guys.

SPC Campos and I watch as the man is carried in. Always interested in observing medical treatment, we move to a window where we can watch the medics and doctors go to work since this particular waltz isn't on our dance card.

After they restrain the man and treat his minor injuries, they begin inserting chest tubes. This procedure is done so the accumulated blood in the chest cavity may be drained, so as not to hinder adequate lung function, for example, a hemothorax. I gather by the increase in his yelling that this man didn't care for the feeling of a scalpel slicing between his ribs and plastic tubing being squeezed in between. After all interventions are made SPC Campos is called to load up the patient in his ambulance to transport him to the flight line for further evacuation.

With all the excitement I care to have for one evening now complete, I make my way down to the tents that are set up for my SCO and Sergeant Major. Tomorrow the operation officially begins, so I figure I should get some rest in case they need an extra set of hands in the aid station.

The next morning I am roused from my sleep by the crackle of radios and the distant booms of U.S. air strikes. The sounds hit my ears before I am fully conscious so I lie there wondering if it is another one of my dreams. The Sergeant Major poked his head in my tent. "Come out and see this Pete!"

I guess I'm not dreaming. I look at my watch through blurry vision, it reads 0455.

I talk my tired body into braving the chilly temperature and going outside. There isn't a whole lot to see from this point. The far off noises of dropping ordinance are rather impressive, so I ask for the reasoning behind the action.

"It's all part of the operation." Sergeant Major Muniz says, in his thick Spanish accent. "Our troops are bombing the shit out of a little piece of land outside of the city to instill a little fear in the bad guys we're going after today."

Makes sense. I guess if I was "Joe Terrorist" nothing would make me think twice about my beliefs more than if I saw the most powerful military in the world firing its most destructive weapons in my backyard. This promises to be an interesting couple of days.

The first day actually passed without incident at the Tiger Aid Station. I heard that quite a few men were rounded up and transferred to an EPW (Enemy Prisoner of War) camp a few miles down the road at another train station by an old phosphate plant. No American casualties so far. I know better than to get my hopes up. Experience tells me that business doesn't pick up in the aid station until after nightfall.

I ask my SCO if I can hang out at the aid station in case they need any extra help. She finds this to be a good idea, so shortly after dinner that evening I proceed up the hill and around the trains.

As I enter the aid station the medics are preparing the trauma room for what might be a busy night. IV bags are neatly hung and spiked. Airway adjunct are readily available and litter teams are assigned. They are short one man at a station so I volunteer.

During a trauma every medic has a distinct job. One transcribes information from the patient or his buddy. One takes vitals and reports to the doc. Another may check any interventions made and apply new dressings or bandages. For tonight, my job is to monitor incoming patient's vitals and keep an ongoing assessment of these vitals so that our doctor will have a good picture of what is going on with the patient.

Stationed at the aid station is a Reserve unit from Kentucky. They are known as a FST (Forward Surgical Team). During this deployment, I have worked with them many times. Their professionalism and knowledgeable staff continue to impress me. I have become good friends with their Head Trauma Nurse. His name is Lieutenant Colonel Ted Henderson.

LTC Henderson and I had spent many nights together playing cards, drinking coffee and discussing politics. His father was a Combat Medic in WWII, so his lineage is steeped in service as is mine. Even though the rank difference is great, he never hesitates to give me advice about nursing school, combat and life itself. It is a beneficial relationship that helps a young Soldier like myself focus on the important task at hand. LTC Henderson and his associates are going to have their work cut out for them tonight.

Just as I sit down to grab a quick bite to eat, we get the call. There was a riot in town and some of our Soldiers are sent there to aid the local police in calming the crowd. Upon arrival, our American

HMMWV drives past an IED that has been set up in anticipation of our response. Three Soldiers are injured, one seriously. We are prepared and unfortunately it is time to begin our night.

In a few short moments our injured HMMWV is pulling up and the most serious casualty brought into the aid station. As they gingerly place him on the litter stands, the smell of blood immediately wafts to my nostrils. My eyes scan the entire length of our patient. His uniform is torn in many places and blood has soaked through his clothing and drips to the floor. The moans of the patient and the shouts of the medical personnel seem like echoes of the Chinook disaster shouting through the caverns of my mind.

I am standing on the left side of the patient. I cut away his shirt and apply the blood pressure cuff. It fits snugly around his muscular arm. I check his pulse and place the pulse oximeter on his finger while I inflate the cuff. Pulse is rapid and weak. Blood pressure is low. *Not a good sign.*

I note the figures and shout them out to the medic transcribing the information. I dance my way around the other medics to the patient's head and check his pupils for responsiveness. His left eye is reactive to light. *Good.* I make my way around to his right side, and that is when I discover the extent of his injuries.

His entire right arm looks like it has been fed into a meat grinder. Bits and pieces of bone are scattered throughout the bloody, jelly-like form that was once his arm. His hand is still intact, fingers twitching slightly. Blood is dripping onto the floor and onto my sand-colored boots.

I ignore the familiar smell of blood and return my attention to his head to observe his right eye. As I focus the light on his pupil,

I am discouraged by what I see. His eye is covered in filth and shrapnel. What is worse, he isn't responding to the light. I ask him if he can see the light. He does not answer. My stomach sinks.

The need for surgery is imminent. Immediate action is needed if we are to save this man's arm, and possibly his eye. All necessary interventions are now made and the doctor clears him for surgery, courtesy of the FST. I say a silent prayer for this wounded warrior, another protector of freedom, as they carry him into the operating room.

As our patient is undergoing surgery for his injuries, I tend to the two other injured Soldiers. Both men have suffered only slight harm from shrapnel. I expose the wounds, extract whatever bits of metal I can and irrigate the wounds.

While I am treating the shrapnel wounds of these two Soldiers, my mind begins to drift. I begin thinking of what has just happened. I didn't freeze. I performed just as I was trained without a single moment of hesitation. Just days ago I worried that I wouldn't be able to perform my duties; and here I am treating my third casualty of the night. I thank God for His strength and guidance. I was proud of myself and all of the members of the medical team that night. It was in that moment that I realized I made my recovery from the horrible events of 02 November, the Chinook tragedy. I had adapted and overcome. I was ready to face the rest of the deployment, no matter what terrors it threw at me.

I found out later that the FST was indeed able to save the injured man's arm. Miraculously, none of the nerves or arteries were damaged. His eye sight was saved as well. Once again I found myself amazed at the impressive strength of military medicine on the field of battle. I should expect nothing less, for it was *our watch*.

CHAPTER EIGHT

Letters To Home

The LORD is my light and my salvation; whom shall I fear? The LORD is the strength of my life; of whom shall I be afraid? When the wicked, even mine enemies and my foes, came upon me to eat up my flesh, they stumbled and fell. Though a host should encamp against me, my heart shall not fear: though war should rise against me, in this will I be confident.
--Psalms 27: 1-3

Perhaps the most important key to a deployed Soldier's success and dedication is his contact with loved ones from home. For me, that meant writing up to six letters a day to my girlfriend and family. The letters that I wrote home while deployed were heartfelt and truthful. It was from these journal letters that this book was conceived. When living daily on the precipice of death, surrounded by the dying of our own Soldiers, always uncertain of the next day's events, one leaves nothing to chance. I learned so much more about the ones who cared for me though their letters.

As a student of history, I love to research the letters of Soldiers from the Civil War era, all the way until present time. I believe that these letters are better indicators of the past than any text book ever written. They provide a first-person account of what happened. Nothing could be more accurate.

My wife Layla and I built a foundation of love and dedication to each other while we were over 7,000 miles apart. When I departed for Iraq, we were unsure of our future together, as we had just barely met. But through constant writing we grew close and eventually, fell in love. As our love grew, we made plans to marry upon my return. Our incredibly long wait came to an end when we were finally (and patriotically!) wed on July 4, 2004. Her patience and support, along with my family and friends brought me through the most difficult year of my life. I would like to present you with some excerpts from the letters I wrote home to give you, the reader, a glimpse into the thoughts of an ordinary Soldier at war.

29 April 2003

Dear Family;

Well, I made it! We are now at 'TAA Rifles' (Tactical Assembly Area) positioned about 15 miles outside Baghdad. I am staying safe and healthy. Not much resistance on the way from Kuwait. Snipers come out at night and take a few shots but that's about it. We are positioned with the 101st Airborne so their helicopters and our Bradleys make for an impressive force. So far Iraq is a lot cooler than Kuwait. It only gets up to 105 degrees during the day and the nights are quite chilly. You can see every star ever created, it's like sleeping in a planetarium. Not too much in the way of landscape.

Not too many animals, a few lizards, dogs and camels. I appreciate your prayers, I will continue to stay safe, I love you all very much!

01 May 2003

Dear Family;

I had a funny experience yesterday. I was sitting in the back of a HMMWV facing to the rear when a local came to the back of the truck looking to steal something. As he grabbed the first item I yelled, "Kiff!" (Stop! In Arabic) and he looked at me, surprised I was there. He froze, wondering if he should take the goods anyway and run off. I raised my rifle and rested it on his chest and calmly repeated my directions. He decided that stealing from me wasn't in the cards today and ran off quickly. I believe I successfully broke the language barrier. Please keep me in your prayers as I am starting to miss home very much. We've been on MRE's for weeks and still no shower yet. Pray that I stay strong and safe in the days to come. I miss you all very much and hope to see you all soon!

20 May 2003

Dear Layla;

I miss you very much. I have only been here a month and it seems like years since I have been with you. I am not sure what lies ahead for me here so please keep me in your prayers. Thank you so much for being patient. I was so happy to learn that you desired to wait for me to return. I think what we have is very special. It takes a strong woman to endure the hardships that you may face. I keep a picture of you in my Kevlar helmet. It is with me always. We are finally at our temporary resting place, Al Asad airbase. The whole base is trashed from whoever occupied this base before we got here. I assume they left in a hurry. Iraqi uniforms and equipment litter the halls of every building. MiG 29 aircraft are scattered about and there are many weapons caches. Old guard towers are scattered about the perimeter.

It is beginning to get very hot, well over 100 degrees during the day. I will write you as often as I can and keep you updated on what we are doing to the best of my knowledge and ability. I am a little scared but through your prayers and faith in me I know I'll be alright. I love reading your letters so please write as often as you can. You will be the first one I call whenever phones are made available to us. I miss you terribly; I can't wait to come home to you!

I wrote these thoughts down on Independence Day, 2003. I was out by the Jordanian border near the town of Ar Rutba. Since the Fourth of July is one of my favorite holidays, I thought it fitting to reflect on the sacrifices of those that served before me.

04 July 2003

I look at where I am - a country full of contempt for me, my uniform, and my flag. I am so far from home, yet memories of it are so close to my heart. I now dwell in a desolate wilderness, which in comparison to the compassion of the enemy seems full of life.

I look at what I'm wearing. This is a uniform of a Soldier. This uniform has been proudly worn by brave men and women before me; life and death all summed up in a piece of clothing. The blood of wounded, dying men now stains my clothing. This is a sad reminder of an empty seat that will never be filled.

I contemplate what I'm thinking. "How am I so fortunate?" I am still alive, unhurt – save the memories of my fellow suffering countrymen. I'll never forget their faces. The expression as life leaves the body is seared into my memory. Their sacrifice isn't in vain. They are the heroes; I ponder their sacrifice on this special day.

I ponder what I'm feeling. I feel pride for my flag and dedication to my brothers in arms. Freedom cannot be explained, it may only be felt. Gratitude to the ones before me, this feeling will always remain with me. I pray that as I follow in their footsteps, I will secure these same freedoms which Americans hold so dear.

02 August 2003

Dear Family;

Well, Happy Birthday to me! Not exactly the celebration I had in mind, but it will have to do for the time being. I'm in Ar Ramadi and aside from the occasional mortar shell falling, it's pretty quiet. Since it's my birthday I wanted to write a "short story" telling you how I spent my last night as a 22-year-old, so here goes. I love you all very much! Keep the mail coming!

***

A few hours after sunset I find myself a comfortable place in the back of my ambulance to try and get some much needed sleep. The heat lies thick on my skin. Every three seconds I swat at the mosquitoes and sand fleas that team up against my comfort. Their unsuccessful comrades that lie smashed and dead on my sticky skin don't seem to deter them at all. Off in the aid station behind me

I hear fellow troopers playing poker. Their game is interrupted by swatting, slapping and swearing at the pests.

I try to ignore them and let my mind drift. My eyes scan the inside of my ambulance. If these litters could talk! They have held the last wishes and words of patriotic heroes. This vehicle has witnessed death and dying along with the medics who worked feverishly to help the wounded cheat death. I can almost hear the ghosts still screaming out or moaning in their pain and sorrow. The memory can sometimes be louder than reality. It just seems to work that way.

As I try to put this out of my mind, I begin to once again swat at the insects bent on destroying my flesh. Sweat stings my eyes and pools in my ears. The thoughts and heat are too much for me, so I move to the top of my vehicle. From here I can see our perimeter, along with every last star God ever hung in the sky. For now it seems I have eluded the mosquitoes and the fleas. But it's only a matter of time before their scouts find me and radio back to HQ about my new location.

I can't sleep. The roaming dogs barking and fighting over a dead rat keeps me awake. It seems this whole town is against the idea of me sleeping tonight. I try something else. I think of my family. I don't dare think of them too long for fear of becoming homesick. I look at my watch, it reads 0200. Sure enough, the insects are back.

A mortar attack should be coming soon. The dogs, buzzing inscects, the dogs, the sweating, the dogs, the swearing and slapping, the dogs ... BOOM! A flash and rumble on our perimeter. BOOM! Another one. I roll off of my vehicle and take cover, weapon ready for action. I wait for the cry of "MEDIC!" I lay low, scanning the direction of the blast. The rattle of automatic gunfire sounds. The sweat stings my eyes. I no longer notice the bugs that have made a playground of my epidermis. RAT-TAT-TAT-TAT! I hear our weapons replying to the mortars. Then as quickly as it began, it ended. Silence. Nothing. I'm watching, listening, waiting. Over the radio I hear, "Trauma 6, Trauma 6, This is Lighting X-Ray, situation tight, out."

I make sure my weapon is back on "safe". I lay down, my heart slows. The dogs, the sweating, the swearing, the slapping. I slap until I get tired of slapping. I get up and make coffee. This country got the best of me tonight. No sleep, but I made it to 23 years old. Thank God.

While in combat, Soldiers have time to reflect on many things that are important to them. They write thoughts and ideas to loved ones that perhaps would have gone unsaid had they not deployed. The following is one of those letters. I like to use many different styles in my writing so I wrote this letter to my family as if I was explaining to a third party how I felt for them.

02 December 2003

Dear Family;

When you are faced with challenges, as we often are in life, one is apt to become pensive. While all together at the same time, confused. During these times of trial I have found myself more and more thankful for the blessing of a loving home.

I remember how my father looked at me after we won a baseball game - with pride. I remember how he looked at me after we lost

- with pride. In fact, as I recall all of the hobbies and endeavors my father and I have undertaken in the past 23 years, I recall nothing but joy, patience and pride. I tried my best to please my father, not for fear of his wrath, but for fear of his disappointment in me. The latter wrenching my heart much more than the former. My father and I have crossed Europe together, spent many stormy nights in tents, and, as odd as it is to say, grown older together. I've found that I will never outgrow his advice. The traits that my sweetheart loves me for now are traits that I have gleaned from my father. As a pastor, he has chosen a life of service, second only to his family. By his example, I have chosen a life of sacrifice. He demonstrated love and respect for my mother as an example for my brother and me to follow. I hope that one day I will become half the man he is.

Behind every selfless action my father displayed for us boys was my mother, a strong woman whose lap and comfort I will never outgrow. As I was growing up, she was the moral beacon through what would have otherwise been the "shipwreck of puberty". Always there in the stands, wearing her sons' faces on buttons with pride, yelling her encouragements for us. Always on her boys' side when it came time to talk my father into putting Christmas lights up on the outside of the house in the blistery Indiana weather. She was the perfect referee for two little boys'scuffles and the pillar of support for our father. These days my visits to home are rare, but she never fails to have one of my favorite meals ready for me. Sacrificing her own time and desires to put me through college, I thank her for providing me with a priceless education. Her closet reveals countless clothing items which represent organizations in which my brother and I have taken part: Baseball teams, Basketball teams, Universities, the Army, and even her yellow ribbon that she wears for me now. Her dedication to God and family is unparalleled. My brother and I always are priority.

My baby brother is now full steam ahead on his way to adulthood as well. Unfortunately, with college and the army, I have missed that transition. It seemed to have passed me by as I was engulfed in my own college education and my adventures with Uncle Sam. I thank God everyday for my brother. His dedication to his studies is an inspiration to me. We are so alike in attributes and activities, yet have incredible differences too. Now in this far away place, I wish I could go back to our Little League days together. Perhaps because that was the last time that I was taller than him! I remember our walks through stores. The girls would always talk to him first, and I was the one trying to look cool. I guess life isn't always fair. From our late night hockey tournaments to early morning hunting expeditions, I cherish every memory. Now on his way to being grown, I only hope he knows that I will always be available, even when I can't physically be there. The bond of brotherhood is beyond love. It is an unspoken truce and treaty, protection of each other until the end.

As I look to complete this chapter of my life, I look to the next with hopes of continuing the tradition of love and respect I have grown up knowing. One day I hope that I am as good at coaching as my father, marry someone as loving and supportive as my mother, and form friendships that will last as long as my bond with my brother. Dad, Mom, Justin: Thank you so much for providing me with the strength I need to perform the awesome task at hand. You at home are my heroes; I love you all!

23 December 2003

Dear Layla,

Hello Sweetheart! As Christmas is only a few days away, I find myself missing you even more. The reality of a year long deployment has set in. I look forward to the day when we no longer spend these special times apart. Thank you again for waiting for me. Wish your family "Happy Holidays" for me. I hope that you all get to spend plenty of time with your family. It looks like we will be home around April sometime. I guess that means we are past the half way point. Stay strong, Sweetie, and keep me in your prayers. I have told you how difficult some of the things are that I have experienced. I pray everyday that God will give me the strength to continue to do my best. We will have so much to discuss when I get home. The future for you and me seems brighter everyday. I will keep sending you letters as I have time between missions. I love you so much! Merry Christmas!

I wrote these thoughts to my family during my first Christmas away from home. The holidays are a rough time for Soldiers to be away from their loved ones. One of the marvels of our brotherhood is how we are able to pull together and be there for each other in these difficult times.

25 December 2003

As my eyes grow heavy from a long day of duty, the whispers of Soldiers still awake flutter in the distance. I roll over and open my eyes. On a little crate in the center of the tent is a pathetic little Christmas tree. Its multi-colored lights were placed with care and they illuminate periodically. This pitiful little symbol would have surely found its way to the 'clearance rack' had someone's family not thought we could use a little holiday cheer on the other side of the world where occasions of cheeriness are few and far between.

In my mind's eye I can picture my family room back home in Indiana. The windows are lined with frost and snow while the warm crackle of the fireplace fills the room with a wonderful scent. The backyard is covered in snow and seeds from the bird feeder lie delicately on its surface. I lick my lips and I can almost taste the peppermint ice cream Mom buys for us every December. I can feel myself drifting to sleep on the family room floor – the end credits to "Rudolf the Red Nosed Reindeer" scroll up the TV screen. I dream of waking to the sounds of my father singing, my mother cooking pancakes, and my brother snoring. How I miss home!

Unwillingly, I bring myself back to reality. Back to my world of sand covered clothes and medical emergencies. My eyes rest once again on the little tree, the only source of light in the tent. This time, it doesn't seem so pathetic. I focus on its little lights reflecting against the rifles that are stacked next to it. I say a heartfelt prayer for you all back home. I then say another prayer for every one of us that have to spend this time away from our families, answering the call to freedom. May God bless us all in this season and may I never take for granted beautiful little Christmas trees like this one.

This letter was sent to me by my mother towards the end of my tour in Iraq. Her faithful prayers for my safety sustained me during my deployment. She wrote one of her prayers down and sent it to me for encouragement. This letter will give you an insight to the pride and fear that a mother feels for her son who is fighting for his country far from home.

04 February 2004

Dear God,

It's 2:00 AM here, 1300 there. I can't sleep. I have to talk to you about my little boy. My heart is overwhelmed with all the precious memories you have given us throughout his life, and the ones we look forward to making when he returns to us.

I'll never forget the way it felt the first time I recognized the movement of new life growing inside me - at first it's like the soft flutter of butterfly wings, then before you know it, he's strong and stretching for more room and then it feels like I am restraining an exploring, tumbling astronaut.

And oh- the softness of a newborn! Softer than the petals of a rose! The nights I sat and rocked my baby while he nursed, rubbed his soft little head, imagined what plans You had for him. And I sang to him about Your loving grace, most often, "The Old Rugged Cross". I remember feeling so privileged to be a part of the bond You have created between mother and child. I remember feeling sorry for dads – that they can never quite fully experience all that You have given to a woman when You honor her with motherhood and allow her to be such a vital part of Your creation.

We had the joyful dedication of his life to You with our church family, but we knew more importantly, that we had already dedicated him to You in our hearts long before the day of that simple ceremony. We had that scare when he was only eight months old! The doctor told us he suspected spinal meningitis. We prayed Psalm 91 over his small, feverish, restless form and clung to You because no one else could comfort us the way You did. We'll never forget the way You touched all of our lives that week when we saw him healed right before our eyes. Just two months later, I was the one back in the hospital with gall bladder disease. The family brought my precious 10-month-old to visit me and I saw him toddle there in the family visiting room for the first time. They all tried their best to lie to me and tell me it was his very first steps, but I knew better. But it was the first steps that I got to see, so that's why it will always be in that room that memories of it remain. Once again, You blessed us as I made a complete recovery.

The bittersweet joy of every September - how I cried the first day of Kindergarten when I had to leave my baby in a new environment where I could not control every situation to be sure his heart would not be broken every day. How each autumn marked the beginning of one less year where he would no longer be fully mine, but yet he was growing to learn more of You. Etched in my memory forever is how he stood straddling his bicycle that September when we pulled away from Taylor University, how I cried to be leaving him once again in an unknown environment and prayed that he would become fully Yours.

Along the way, there were of course, many things I wish I could do over. Many times I spoke the wrong words in haste or didn't take time to ask You what I should do. Probably even times when I was causing hurt to the child I so desperately wanted to protect from all hurt. Times when I should have been a better example of your love and forgiveness so that the child You gave me would see more of his Heavenly Father, and less of the failings of his earthly mother. I know that You have forgiven me of those times, and I know my children have too, Lord, and I thank You if I am the only one who remembers them.

Now, more than ever, Lord, I need You so desperately. Now, more than ever, Lord, my child is so much further from my protective embrace than he's ever been. And in so much more danger than he's ever known or I could ever imagine. And just like we did when he was a baby of eight months, we look to You because You are the only One Who can protect him and comfort us. You are the only One Who can help him feel our daily prayers surrounding him even when the mail has not yet arrived or the phone call cannot go through.

Right now Lord, I pray for my child, my son, who will always be a child in my eyes. Keep him safe from the enemy who desires to hurt him. Keep his thoughts and mind on You. Give him the strength to be a comfort to the wounded. Heal all the wounds that war wages on the human mind, body, and spirit. Heal all the sights, sounds, and smells in his memory that a young man was never meant to have to experience. Have Your hand upon him every day in every way. Amen

This was the letter that I wrote to Layla describing how strongly I felt about our future together. While I was away, Layla and I came to know each other through letters and occasional phone calls. Her strength, dedication and love for me solidified in my heart the desire to spend the rest of my life with the woman I had fallen in love with over 7,000 miles away.

14 February 2004

Dear Layla;

Hello sweetheart! Well, I am only two months away from coming home now. We have made it so far together. I thank you so much for your support in the most difficult time of my life. You have been the strong pillar that I could always lean on. The past year has brought many trials to both of us. I think that what you and I have is so special. I have come to love a beautiful, compassionate woman in the midst of hatred and war. I write to tell you now that I want to spend the rest of my life with you by my side. I can think of nothing else that would complete my life as your love. We will have many more opportunities to discuss this in the future, but we both know that no time is better than the present to tell each other our feelings. I love you so much and I could not bear the thought of ever living without you. I dream of you day and night and long for the day I will be with you again. I will write as much as I can with the busy months that are ahead. Please stay faithful in your prayers. I love you, I'll be home soon.

15 March 2004

Dear Family;

Well, I've made it. Our entire Regiment is now at Camp Victory, Kuwait. In less than two weeks I'll be home. It seems this past year has gone quickly now that I look back at it. Many times I sat and prayed for you all as I sat in the middle of the desert dreaming of returning home again. I feel like I have grown so much in the past year. I guess the sights and sounds of a country torn by terrorism and violence will make you grow up in a hurry. Thank you so much for your prayers. God's angels have come to my aid on more than one occasion and for that I am very thankful.

I can hardly wait to come home to Indiana. It seems I spent the last 23 years of my life trying to get out of Indiana, now I have spent the last year praying for the day that I would return. The cornfields don't seem as dull and the quietness of our neighborhood is something I truly cherish now more than ever.

Thank you so much for being there for Layla. She has relied on you all so much in the past year. I plan on asking her to marry me when I come home in April. I believe that the love and patience that is formed and tried in these circumstances has a good fighting chance against anything the world may throw at us from here on.

As I prepare to leave, I feel a sense of pride, yet sadness. I am proud that I had my chance to serve my country in its efforts to protect freedom for others. I am sad to be leaving, as odd as that may sound. I have grown up here for the past year of my life. I have lost friends and formed friendships. I have seen mankind at his worst, and at the same time, I have witnessed selflessness and courage that I have never known.

Thank you all again so much for everything that you have done for me. I am convinced that without your strength for me back home, I would not be able to write you with such a positive outlook. There are already plans of us returning in a year. I ask that you stay strong and trust in God Above that I will come home to you safely once again should we return for another tour. I cannot wait to see you all. I love you so much!

CHAPTER NINE

For the Veterans

I wrote this poem a few months after returning home. It is written from the perspective of a father who served in Viet Nam and never received the greeting he deserved upon returning home. His son is now fighting in Iraq and he is dedicated to welcome his boy home in the fashion that he himself deserved, but never received.

The "Welcome Home" that I received placed wonderful feelings in my heart. As friends and family waited for me at the airport, I got to see first hand all of the Americans that had prayed for us and our safe return. It moved me so much that I was left pondering how those who returned home from war in the 60's and 70's could ever possibly cope. Their strength through one of the most difficult periods of America's history is an inspiration to me. It is the American veteran that inspires this book and my dedication to service. Therefore, if you are an American veteran and you never received the thanks that is due you, this book is in honor of you. Thank you for guarding America under *your watch*! Welcome Home!

Welcome Home

When I went away, as just a boy, not yet a man
They taught me how to kill in the jungles of Viet Nam
This ruck sack on my back and rifle in my hands
Standing tall, back to the wall, for good 'ol Uncle Sam

Bullets raised me fast; you could see it in my eyes
The things I'd seen and what I'd done took me by surprise
I never laughed; God only knows you'd never see me cry
I served my flag with honor, tho' death toll on the rise

My brethren fell like rain drops in cold September skies
For the cause of freedom they all gave their lives
I hid my tears so long ago, now I shed them every day
Always on my mind are their deaths of yesterday

When I came home to the land I love
No one was waiting, nobody to hug
No mommy, no daddy to see how I'd grown
No one to hold me or kiss me or welcome me home

Now my boy stands tall, off fighting in the sands
Protecting all our freedoms in far, unfriendly lands
I long to get him back, to see how much he's grown
I'll hold him and kiss him and tell him "Welcome Home"

When they all get home to the land they love
Be that person waiting so they'll have someone to hug
They've all done and seen things - some we'll never know
Just hold them and tell them how you love them so
"Welcome Home"

CHAPTER TEN

A Love from 7,000 Miles Away

Layla A. Peters

My husband and I had only just met and been dating a little over a month before he left for Iraq. Joshua told me shortly before he left that he was not sure what to do about starting a relationship with me, as he was frightened at the thought of what could happen to him over there. Once we decided to continue our relationship in spite of the circumstances, I had never been so happy to know that he was willing to follow his faith and pursue a serious relationship. I knew after that short time of dating Joshua that I wanted to spend the rest of my life with him.

Joshua arrived in Kuwait for 'Operation Iraqi Freedom' on April 1st, 2003. I had never felt so alone and scared. I was still living with my parents at the time, so having them immediately available for comfort was a blessing. However, I did not know exactly what direction to take in life, as I had just graduated from Indiana University and was searching for a career.

I remember the last telephone conversation Joshua and I had the night he departed from Fort Carson, Colorado. We had not seen each other since mid-March. He sounded very brave and determined, but little did I know at the time how frightened he was of the unknown. I believe he was doing everything in his power during that conversation to keep me from worrying, and likewise, I was saying everything in my power to encourage him. The moment we hung up the phone I began to cry. I did not know when I was to hear from him again, or even if I was ever going to see him again and that truly upset me.

Time went by very slowly after he deployed. I knew I was going to write Joshua letters, but at the time I was still uncertain about his feelings for me and did not want to scare him away. I decided to write him only once a week so he would not be bombarded with letters.

I prayed for Joshua constantly. Whenever I was feeling discouraged, I would drive to the War Memorial Park in my hometown and just sit and pray. I read the passages on the wall from veterans of World War II and Vietnam to gain a sense of inspiration and hope. Some days were harder than others. Some days I would just sit and cry at the thought of him being in harm's way, as hard as I tried not to dwell on the unknown. I kept re-assuring myself that he was doing a job that needed to be done. I had to believe that he was staying safe and making the right decisions.

I never thought that my favorite part of the day would be checking the mailbox. I looked forward to the afternoon when the mailman came as each day passed, which kept me going. I kept saying to myself, "this could be the day I hear from Joshua."

One day, I was gardening with my parents when the mail truck came. I had finally gotten a letter from Joshua! I think the entire neighborhood heard me rejoicing as I tore open his letter. The letter was short and to the point. Joshua portrayed fatigue most of all, as he had been awake for over seventy hours straight due to the extreme schedule of getting settled into Kuwait. I was so elated that day. It had taken over a month for me to receive my first communication from him.

Soon after that, things began coming together in my life. I had just accepted a position as a news reporter for a radio station in Kokomo, Indiana. My dreams were beginning to come true. I had a passion for Joshua and a purpose in my career goals.

Reporting the news was not an easy task. Aside from writing local stories, I referred to the Associated Press news wire for state and national stories. Before my job gave me access to news, I had previously been glued to the "war on television." I had formed quite a relationship with Fox News, especially Shepherd Smith. Everyday, I felt a sense of comfort to have that connection with Joshua through his coverage of the war. As a news reporter myself, I had access to the national news from sources such as Reuters, etc. I cringed each day while checking the news at work, knowing the love of my life was in the midst of that madness.

In the following weeks and months, I sent Joshua a package of "goodies" every two weeks. About a month and a half after his deployment, he was able to call me. It was surreal. I could not believe I was actually hearing his voice. That was when I realized how distant we were from one another. There was a bad connection on the satellite phone and the relay time was over three seconds. However, I did remember him saying, "Please write me more letters."

I immediately responded. I would write him at least once a day instead of once a week. I would tell him everything that was on my mind. Since Joshua and I did not know each other very well before he left, we got to know each other much better through our correspondence.

Just as Joshua and I did not know much about one another, I had never met his parents or anyone else in his family. I took the initiative to meet his family soon after he deployed and eventually developed a very tight and loving relationship with his parents. His parents and I kept in contact and informed one another of any new communication. I made it a point to keep in touch with his parents. It was actually very comforting to have a connection with them because I felt that much closer to Joshua.

I also made it my mission to make Joshua's life in Iraq more comfortable and livable. However, I knew that would be a challenge. I asked him if he needed anything. If he needed deodorant, I sent him deodorant. If he needed a shower, I actually sent him a portable shower. We even tape recorded messages to each other on miniature voice recorders. I sang to him and put music to poems that he sent me. One special request from Joshua holds meaning still today. He told me that he wanted a chain necklace of Saint Michael to remind him of God's protection in times of battle. My father and I found exactly what he wanted, as we all knew of his recent strife.

The Saint Michael was en route to the Middle East on the day of the November 2nd Chinook tragedy. Joshua was finally scheduled to go on a Rest and Relaxation trip for a few days. I was so very happy for him, as he deserved a break to say the least. The day of the helicopter crash was the worst day of all. There had been other previous close calls during his missions, but this incident in particular tried my faith. I had never prayed so much in my life. I had never been so afraid. It was a day of confusion and conflicting stories. The news on television was giving inconsistent reports, as well as the AP wire at my radio statioin to which I was adhering. Forty-eight hours later, I finally heard from my Joshua. He recounted the story to me through his tears and we cried together. I had never been so happy to hear his voice and to finally know that he was okay.

From that point on, my perspective changed. I was thankful to get to hear from him whenever he could call and I had absolute faith that he would come home safely. I truly believe that the Lord had spared Joshua's life to save the Soldiers in the other helicopter. I thank God everyday for Joshua and the future we will get to share.

I continued to keep my faith through the holidays and into the New Year. I devoted my life to be with Joshua spiritually as I knew he was going through a very difficult time. We were able to communicate more often as phone centers were made available to troops. We both knew that his redeployment back to the States was near and we were soon to be reunited.

In April of 2004, Joshua came home from the war in Iraq. I was so proud of his dedication and service to our country. To my surprise, he proposed to me a month after being home and we were married on the Fourth of July, 2004. I would never have imagined a love could grow from 7,000 miles away. I cannot wait to spend the rest of my life with him. I love Joshua with all my heart.

Mr. and Mrs. Joshua Peters on their wedding day, July 4th, 2004.

CHAPTER ELEVEN

A Child ... A Father ... An American

Timothy A. Peters

Growing up during the late 1960's and early 1970's, a small part of innocence was stolen from the childhoods of small town America. The Vietnam War was at its apex and the conflict, with it savage footage of war, enveloped us each evening as we sat around the dinner table watching the daily news. For the first time in American history, the carnage, terror, and sadness of war was delivered directly into our homes. For the first time our country had to deal with polarizing opinions concerning an overseas conflict which many times spilled over into the streets of our own neighborhoods where non-uniformed Americans were also injured or killed.

During a time when banners were being raised to celebrate mankind's first step on the surface of the moon, the banner most vivid to me were the ones with a blue star in the middle, prominently displayed in the front windows of homes, which to my childish mind, seemed to be randomly chosen.

I began to understand the meaning of the starred banners when their loved ones returned home from their tours of duty. The survivors who returned home were different. Having left a homeland of relative peace and quiet where it is natural to be friendly and even optimistic, they returned harder in their demeanor and less tolerant of those neighbors who had remained untouched by the life-and-death issues that these Soldiers had dealt with on a daily basis. It seemed as though they were always on edge and it was to one's advantage to choose his words or actions a little more cautiously while around them.

As I watched my community change, nothing affected me as much as a conversation I overheard my father have with one of my younger brothers. While in high school, my thoughts were of the job I might have when I graduated because I knew there was no money to attend college. It never occurred to me that those images I watched each evening on the news or the starred banners hanging in windows down our street, or the hardened neighbors would come so close to touching my life. Not knowing that I could hear them, my father told my brother that I would probably be drafted when I graduated from high school and go to Vietnam. Suddenly the reality of it all was up close and personal and that frightening possibility that now existed never left my mind.

Thankfully, for me, the Vietnam War ended and all of the troops were evacuated just before I graduated. The feelings I had during those years never left me and continued to follow me into my adult life. Now married, and the father of two sons, I never ceased to pray that my children would never see the division of their country as I had during the 1970's or experience war.

I have always been proud of my children; their accomplishments in high school and college had indeed given me cause to celebrate and yes, even partake in a few button-popping brag sessions. I had the privilege of being their baseball and basketball coach. We hunted, fished, camped, and hiked together. We traveled to different countries together and served in charitable missions together. We developed a bond that goes beyond a father/son relationship and includes the title of best friends. My sons have never caused me grief and they spared me the frustration of teenage rebellion. When my elder son graduated from college, my dreams of him finding his special someone to marry and settling down in a good job now seemed certain. September 11, 2001 changed all that.

My wife and I had taken a small trip to celebrate our 25th wedding anniversary when our son called to tell us he would be raising his right hand for Uncle Sam. He then began a journey through the Army's "alphabet soup," receiving titles I never expected to hear; SPC Joshua Peters of the United States Army; Combat Medic with the 3d ACR; and a deployed Soldier to the country of Iraq.

The following year was the hardest year of my life. Events that you have read about in this book brought many anxious days and sleepless nights. I was now consumed by as much news as I could get and lived from letter to letter, checking the mailbox in great anticipation every single day. I became thankful to hear the phone ringing in the middle of the night, as it was mid-morning of his day when given a chance to call. It mattered not if the phone call had static or a four second delay; we heard his voice and had one more chance to say "I love you" at least one more time. We at least knew on that day in that moment he was alive and well. I also lived from prayer to prayer and on promises from God's Word for my son's protection.

The emotions during that year were difficult to hold back, though I'm sure I did not always succeed. When I heard of soldiers being deployed, I cried. When I heard of soldiers coming home, I cried. When I heard of soldiers being killed, I cried. When I heard of wounded soldiers even missing limbs wanting to return to their units, I cried. When I thought of the things my son was witnessing and the thought of evil people far away wanting to kill him, I cried. So many times I ached with the pain of holding back emotions publicly. But during all of this, I was proud of my son and the job he was doing. He was trained, he was mature, and he had risen to the challenges before him.

Our darkest day was indeed November 2, 2003. We knew our son was scheduled for R&R, and that morning as I was watching one of the headline news channels, across the bottom of the screen the story scrolled of two Chinook helicopters heading out for R&R shot down . . . and I knew. I immediately turned off the television because I did not want my wife to know until we could receive direct word. I waited throughout the day for some news, and prayed. Finally at 3:00 p.m. that afternoon I received a phone call from an officer in Iraq. When he identified himself, my breathing stopped and my heart raced. At the beginning of his communication, I had no idea what news he had for us. By now you have read the account of that tragic day, told first hand by my courageous son, Specialist Joshua Peters.

It is amazing how countless citizens came to our side during that year and offered everything from moral support to prayers to care packages. Words alone could not possibly express the gratitude I feel. My greatest comfort came from a passage of Scripture from my Bible. *Psalm 91:2, 9-11 - . . . My God, in Him will I trust. Because thou hast made the Lord, which is my refuge, even the most High, thy habitation; There shall no evil befall thee, neither shall any plague come nigh they dwelling. He shall give his angels charge over thee, to keep thee in all thy ways.* This was a promise that I read and prayed every day.

My wife and I were there when Joshua returned to his post at Fort Carson, Colorado. When his group was officially dismissed, we three found each other in the sea of desert uniforms. No words could be spoken, only the tears and the sounds of the emotions of the past year as they were squeezed out in a long and much overdue embrace.

I am thankful for men and women like my son who have answered the call to defend the principles of our country. To this day I never hesitate to shake the hand of a man or woman in uniform and thank them for the job they are doing. I have often said that I did not raise my children to experience war or its effects . . . however, I did raise them to serve. It is that dedication to serve that makes me the proud father of a Combat Medic, a proud American supporting our men and women around the world, and has given me greater understanding of what I experienced as a child in that small rural community.

There is a banner with a blue star hanging with pride in my front window. There is a flag pole in the front yard with an American flag waving; ready to be replaced at the first sign of wear or tattered ends. There is a greater love for every veteran of every war deep within my heart. There are daily, fervent prayers offered in my home for those who wear this nation's sacred honor and uniform into battle. Combat Medic Specialist Joshua M. Peters is responsible for all of that.

I challenge each reader to continue to pray for our great homeland and our nation's leaders, to be supportive of our Soldiers who stand ready, and to take the opportunity to let this mission also be *your watch*.

---SECTION THREE---

A Hope for the World

Our lifetime will forever be bookmarked by the attacks of September 11th 2001. Timelines in conversations are based on "Hey, remember when........ before September 11th?" Terror has been brought under a microscope and its networks have been the focus of a world that will not tolerate it. Everyone and everything has been affected. A call was issued for all who oppose terror to stand up and fight. The world is the 21st century battle ground. Businesses were challenged to continue to grow, proving that terror would not hinder production. World leaders were challenged to cut any ties with terror based on funding, aiding, or protecting with the promise of swift action against them should they not comply. Citizens of the globe were put to the test of never allowing terror to rule their lives. Militaries were deployed to ensure a bright future for countries whose freedoms were taken by extremists. Sometimes it takes darkness for there to be a light.

Terror will not win. Fear will not rule. Everyday that passes unveils new progress in the global war on terror. We, along with the rest of our military brothers and sisters, have personally witnessed the progress of our efforts to restore hope and peace in lands that once knew only oppression.

This progress is not known to many unless you have witnessed it firsthand. We have seen countless towns receive electricity and clean water for the first time in decades. We have seen people finally live without the fear of a tyrant who sought to destroy them at the slightest hint of insubordination. We saw them rejoice in the streets when his capture was made public. We have seen children going to school using supplies that were donated by global citizens and distributed by Coalition Soldiers.

We have seen patriotism and valor. The sort of valor that is only read about in textbooks, we have seen with our own eyes. This valor surpasses all human reasoning and understanding. This valor in men's hearts would lead them to lay down their lives in the stead of their brethren. We have patriotism in our hearts that perhaps hasn't been felt by many people since this glorious nation's Greatest Generation saved the world over 60 years ago. This patriotism leads us to salute our flag with a precious respect and a cognitive understanding for the cost of freedom.

We have seen courage and sacrifice. Courage that is unparalleled and unmatched by any suicide bomber or fundamentalist. Sacrifice that when contemplated, brings tears to our eyes and a sense of pride in our hearts. We are proud to wear the uniform that so many of our brothers and sisters wore on their last day on earth.

Different cultures and creeds have come together to face a common enemy. We have fought alongside other Soldiers who wear different flags on their sleeves, but a unified purpose in their hearts. These other Coalition Soldiers have realized as we have, that there still remains a very real threat. This threat cannot be taken lightly.

We've asked ourselves why we continue to do what we do. Our answer is simple; we do not want our children living in a new cold war era. We do not want the future to bow to the fanatical ideals of a few radicals planning doomsday plots in a bunker funded by corruption. No matter what information is made public and what information is kept silent, we know the truth in our hearts because we have been there. We are proud to be part of the force that will not sit idly by and let evil and terror rule. We are proud to be serving in the forces that defend this great nation and the cause of freedom. We are proud to be part of a force that has brought freedom to millions. And most of all, we are proud to be Americans.

Every freedom loving person in the world cringes at the thought of losing their God given rights. There is sacrifice involved when freedom is threatened. Nations across this globe have understood these sacrifices and said, "Enough is enough". The world has risen up and proclaimed not now, not ever, *not on my watch*.

Lessons Learned

We again asked ourselves the question that was posed earlier in the book, "If the media had the involvement in World War II like they do in war today, would the allies have won?" The answer simply is, *YES*. Our resolve cannot be conquered. Our fortitude can not be questioned. Our cause for freedom and democracy, and the rights to life, liberty, and the pursuit of happiness for all is just and unbiased.

Should you find yourself ever questioning the reasons for going to war or the politics that drive the war, please never question the drive and determination of the Soldier, Sailor, Airman, or Marine fighting that war. We have been there with these fine service men and women who have sacrificed so much to provide Americans with the freedoms that they enjoy everyday.

The 21st Century is a time of drastic change. The lines of war are not as black and white as they once were. Combat is no longer a uniformed military force fighting another uniformed military force for the control of a hill top or trail. This new age of intelligence means internet spy ware and inside moles coupled with satellites and communication taps. Standard operating procedures change day-to-day to combat enemy techniques. The Soldier is caught in the middle trying to effectively perform the duty he was sent to do. The 21st Century Combat Medic constantly finds himself adapting to ever-changing missions. The 21st Century Combat Medic is the best equipped and best trained medic in the regular Army's history. The demand placed on us pushes us to be the absolute best. We will accept nothing besides the best. No patient will ever get second-class care; not now, not ever, *not on our watch.*

Roll Call

Loss of Task Force 1/504 PIR (Parachute Infantry Regiment) during 'Operation Enduring Freedom'

July 2002-Janurary/Feburary 2003

SGT Steven A. Checko   D Company, 1/504 PIR

Losses of the Third Armored Cavalry Regiment and Attachments during 'Operation Iraqi Freedom I'

April 2003-April 2004

PFC Mack J. Vorn   HHT, First Squadron, 3d ACR

1LT Michael Adams   A Troop, First Squadron, 3d ACR

SGT Michael E. Dooley   B Troop, First Squadron, 3d ACR

SSG Daniel Bader   ADA Battery, First Squadron, 3d ACR

SPC Brian H. Penisten	ADA Battery, First Squadron, 3d ACR
SSG Andrew R. Pokorny	ADA Battery, First Squadron, 3d ACR
CPT Joshua T. Byers	HHT, Second Squadron, 3d ACR
SPC Stephen M. Scott	HHT, Second Squadron, 3d ACR
SGT Thomas F. Broomhead	E Troop, Second Squadron, 3d ACR
SSG William T. Latham	E Troop, Second Squadron, 3d ACR
SSG Michael B. Quinn	E Troop, Second Squadron, 3d ACR
PFC Justin W. Pollard	G Troop, Second Squadron, 3d ACR
PFC Jesse A. Givens	H Company, Second Squadron, 3d ACR
SPC Darius T. Jennings	HOW Battery, Third Squadron, 3d ACR
PV2 Benjamin L. Freeman	K Troop, Third Squadron, 3d ACR
SSG Frederick L. Miller Jr.	K Troop, Third Squadron, 3d ACR
PFC Armondo Soriano	HOW Battery, Third Squadron, 3d ACR
CW2 Matthew Laskowski	O Troop, Fourth Squadron, 3d ACR

CW2 Stephen Wells	O Troop, Fourth Squadron, 3d ACR
SPC Michael A. Diraimondo	571st Medical Co, Fourth Squadron, 3d ACR
SPC Christopher A. Golby	571st Medical Co, Fourth Squadron, 3d ACR
CW2 Hans N. Gukeisen	571st Medical Co, Fourth Squadron, 3d ACR
SGT Richard A. Carl	571st Medical Co, Fourth Squadron, 3d ACR
CW2 Phillip A. Johnson	571st Medical Co, Fourth Squadron, 3d ACR
CW2 Ian D. Manuel	571st Medical Co, Fourth Squadron, 3d ACR
CW3 Brian K. Van Dusen	571st Medical Co, Fourth Squadron, 3d ACR
SGT Earnest G. Bucklew	HHT, Support Squadron, 3d ACR
MAJ Matthew E. Schram	HHT, Support Squadron, 3d ACR
SGT Tamarra J. Ramos	MED Troop, Support Squadron, 3d ACR
SPC Rian C. Ferguson	S & T Troop, Support Squadron, 3d ACR
SGT Taft V. Williams	MAINT Troop, Support Squadron, 3d ACR

SSG Stephen A. Bertolino

AVIM Troop, Support Squadron, 3d ACR

Spencer T. Karol

E Company (LRSD), 51st IN (ABN)

SGT Joel Perez

A Battery, 2nd BN, 5th Field Artillery

SSG Joe N. Wilson

A Battery, 2nd BN, 5th Field Artillery

SGT Keelan L. Moss

B Battery, 2nd BN, 5th Field Artillery

SPC Steven D. Conover

C Battery, 2nd BN, 5th Field Artillery

SPC Rafael L. Navea

C Battery, 2nd BN, 5th Field Artillery

SGT Ross A. Pennanen

C Battery, 2nd BN, 5th Field Artillery

SGT Paul F. Fisher

F Company, 106th Aviation Battalion

1LT Brian D. Slavenas

F Company, 106th Aviation Battalion

CW4 Bruce A. Smith

F Company, 106th Aviation Battalion

SGT Paul F. Velazquez

F Company, 106th Aviation Battalion

PFC Karina S. Lau

B Company, 16th Signal Battalion

PFC Anthony D. D'Agostino	D Company, 16th Signal Battalion
SSG Richard S. Eaton, Jr.	B Company, 323d MI BN, 205th MI BDE
SPC Francis M. Vega	1st Platoon, 151st AG Company (Postal)
PFC James A. Chance III	C Company, 890th Engineer Battalion
PFC David M. Kirchoff	2133d Transportation Company
SPC Aaron J. Sissel	2133d Transportation Company

Glossary

AIT: *advanced individual training.* The school that Soldiers attend after Basic Training which trains them in their job, or MOS.

ATLS: *advanced trauma life support.* Medical equipment found in an aid station that is used to treat most trauma related injuries.

BVM: *bag valve mask.* Medical equipment used to ventilate patients.

CLS: *combat lifesaver.* A non-medical Soldier who is trained by medical personnel to provide basic life saving techniques.

CP: *command post, command point.* A location which houses the planning and logistical capabilities of a unit.

CSH: *combat support hospital.* A mobile hospital that is deployed to locations that support large troop activity with ER and advanced trauma capabilities.

CVC: *combat vehicle communications:* Speaker and microphone system inside of a combat helmet that is used for communication between crew members. This equipment is used in tracked vehicles.

FLA: *front line ambulance, field litter ambulance.* The two types include a two berth and a four berth patient compartment mounted on a HMMWV frame.

FOB: *forward operating base.* A permanent location where military elements may launch strategic missions.

FST: *forward surgical team.* A team of surgeons, doctors, nurses and medics that deploy in support of a larger medical group.

HMMWV: *high mobility multi-purpose wheeled vehicle.* Four wheeled military vehicle also known as the Humvee.

IED: *improvised explosive device.* Any sort of munitions set to discharge from either a hand or remote detonation device. Often found on convoy routes.

LMTV: *light mobile tactical vehicle.* A four wheeled military truck used mostly for transportation of supplies and Soldiers. Comparable in size to the 2 ½ ton truck.

LRS: *long range surveillance.* A team or squad who gathers information and executes attacks from behind enemy lines.

LSA: *logistical staging area:* A location occupied by the military to support troop movements.

MAS: *main aid station.* The primary aid station for a Squadron.

MOS: *military occupational specialty.* The specific job that a Soldier performs. (i.e. infantryman, transportation specialist, healthcare specialist).

MRE: *meal ready to eat.* A compact meal that is issued to troops by the military during field or combat environments.

MTS: *mobile tracking system.* A global positioning computer mounted inside a vehicle with a real-time instant messenger to a command center.

M113-A3: *armored personnel carrier, tracked ambulance.* Armored vehicle used to carry personnel and/or evacuate casualties. Ambulance has four litter berths.

NVG: *night vision goggles.* Equipment that enables Soldiers to conduct missions in little to no light situations.

PA: *physician's assistant.* A highly-trained medical officer that works closely with medics and assumes command of an aid station.

TAA: *tactical assembly area.* A designated area where combat element movements are tracked, re-supplied, and assembled.

TC: *tank commander.* Soldier within a military vehicle that is in charge of navigation and assumes command of the vehicle.

TCP: *traffic control point.* A military check point devised to search vehicles and confiscate contraband.

QRF: *quick reaction force.* A team or squad that is always on alert to handle military emergencies outside of the perimeter.

About The Authors

Joshua Peters is the recipient of the Combat Medic Badge, and two Army Commendation Medals, one with Valor Device for actions during the attack on the CH-47 Chinook Helicopter on 02 November 03. He has been honored with a tribute to Heroism in the Congressional Record of the 108th Congress.

Josh Fansler is the recipient of the Combat Medic Badge in Operation Enduring Freedom and Operation Iraqi Freedom. He has been awarded two Army Commendations Medals for meritorious service. He also possesses the Expert Field Medical Badge and Airborne Wings.

Their published works include the newspapers and magazine of Taylor University, the newsletter Brave Rifles, the magazine American Working Dogs, and the book A Salute to Service by Mike Radford.

DATE DUE

Demco

Made in the USA
Columbia, SC
22 May 2019